EPA 608 Exam Success

By Lewis Morris

Copyright © Network4Learning, Inc. 2018.

www.insiderswords.com/EPA608

ISBN-13:978-1728839219

Table of Contents

Introduction	5
Crossword Puzzles	24
Multiple Choice	64
Matching	86
Word Search	110

What is "Insider Language"?

Recent research has confirmed what we have known for decades: The strongest students and leaders in industry have a mastered an Insider Language in their subject and field. This Insider language is made up of the technical terms and vocabulary necessary to communicate effectively in classes or the workplace. For those who master it, learning is easier, faster, and much more enjoyable.

Most students who are surveyed report that the greatest challenge to any course of study is learning the vocabulary. When we examine typical college courses, we discover that there is, on average, 250 Insider Terms a student must learn over the course of a semester. Further, most exams rely heavily on this set of words for assessment purposes. The structure of multiple choice exams lends itself perfectly to the testing of this Insider Language. Students who can differentiate between Insider Language terms can handle challenging exam questions with ease and confidence.

From recent research on learning and vocabulary we have learned:

- Your knowledge of any subject is contained in the content-specific words you know. The more of these terms that you know, the easier it is to understand and recall important information; the easier it will be to communicate your ideas to peers, professors, supervisors, and co-workers. The stronger your content-area vocabulary is, the higher your scores will be on your exams and written assignments.

- Students who develop a strong Insider Language perform better on tests, learn faster, retain more information, and express greater satisfaction in learning.

- Familiarizing yourself with subject-area vocabulary before formal study (pre-learning) is the most effective way to learn this language and reap the most benefit.

- The vocabulary on standardized exams come directly from the stated objectives of the test-makers. This means that the vocabulary found on standardized exams is predictable. Our books focus on this vocabulary.

- Most multiple-choice exams are glorified vocabulary quizzes. Think about the format of a multiple-choice question. The question stem is a definition of a term and the choices (known as distractors) are 4 or 5 similar words. Your task is to differentiate between the meanings of those terms and choose the correct word.

- It takes a person several exposures to a new word to be able to use it with confidence in conversation or in writing. You need to process these words several different ways to make them part of your long-term memory.

5

The goals of this book are:
- To give you an "Insider Language" for your subject.
- Pre-teach the most important words before you set out on a traditional course of review or study.
- Teach you the most important words in your subject area.
- Teach you strategies for learning subject-area words on your own.
- Boost your confidence in your ability to master this language and support you in your study.
- Reduce the stress of studying and provide you with fun activities that work.

How it works:

The secret to mastering Insider Language is through repetition and exposure. We have eleven steps for you to follow:

1. Read the word and definition in the glossary out loud. "See it, Say it"
2. Identify the part of speech the word belongs to such as noun, verb, adverb, or adjective. This will help you group the word and identify similar words.
3. Place the word in context by using it in a sentence. Write this sentence down and read it aloud.
4. Use "Chunking" to group the words. Make a diagram or word cloud using these groups.
5. Make connections to the words by creating analogies.
6. Create mnemonics that help you recognize patterns and orders of words by substituting the words for more memorable items or actions.
7. Examine the morphology of the word, that is, identify the root, prefix, and suffix that make up the word. Identify similar and related words.
8. Complete word games and puzzles such as crosswords and word searches.
9. Complete matching questions that require you to differentiate between related words.
10. Complete Multiple-choice questions containing the words.
11. Create a visual metaphor or "memory cartoon" to make a mental picture of the word and related processes.

By completing this word study process, you will be exposed to the terminology in various ways that will activate your memory and create a lasting understanding of this language.

The strategies in this book are designed to make you an independent expert at learning insider language. These strategies include:

- Verbalizing the word by reading it and its definition aloud ("See It, Say It"). This allows you to make visual, auditory, and speech connections with its meaning.

- Identifying the type of word (Noun, verb, adverb, and adjective). Making this distinction helps you understand how to visualize the word. It helps you "chunk" the words into groups, and gives you clues on how to use the word.

- Place the word in context by using it in a sentence. Write this sentence down and read it aloud. This will give you an example of how the word is used.

- "Chunking". By breaking down the word list into groups of closely related words, you will learn them better and be able to remember them faster. Once you have group the terms, you can then make word clouds using a free online service. These word clouds provide visual cues to remembering the words and their meanings.

- Analogies. By creating analogies for essential words, you will be making connections that you can see on paper. These connections can trigger your memory and activate your ability to use the word in your writing as you begin to use them. Many of these analogies also use visual cues. In a sense, you can make a mental picture from the analogy.

- Mnemonics. A device such as a pattern of letters, ideas, or associations that assists in remembering something. A mnemonic is especially useful for remembering the order of a set of words or the order of a process.

- Morphology. The study of word roots, prefixes, and suffixes. By examining the structure of the words, you will gain insight into other words that are closely related, and learn how to best use the word.

- Visual metaphors. This is the most sophisticated and entertaining strategy for learning vocabulary. Create a "memory cartoon" using one or more of the vocabulary terms. This activity triggers the visual part of your memory and makes fast, permanent, imprints of the word on your memory. By combining the terms in your visual metaphor, you can "chunk" the entire set of vocabulary terms into several visual metaphors and benefit from the brain's tendency to group these terms.

The activities in this book are designed to imprint the words and their meanings in your memory in different ways. By completing each activity, you will gain the necessary exposures to the word to make it a permanent part of your vocabulary. Each activity uses a different part of your memory. The result is that you will be comfortable using these words and be able to tell the difference between closely related words. The activities include:

A. Crossword Puzzles and Word Searches- These are proven to increase test scores and improve comprehension. Students frequently report that they are fun and engaging, while requiring them to analyze the structure and meaning of the words.

B. Matching- This activity is effective because it forces you to differentiate between many closely related terms.

C. Multiple Choice- This classic question format lends itself to vocabulary study perfectly. Most exams are in this format because they are simple to make, easy to score, and are a reliable type of assessment. (Perfect for the Vocabulary Master!) One strategy to use with multiple choice questions that enhance their effectiveness is to cover the answer choices while you read the question. After reading the question, see if you can answer it before looking at the choices. Then look at the choices to see if you match one of them.

Conducting a thorough "word study" of your insider language will take time and effort, but the rewards will be well worth it. By following this guide and completing the exercises thoughtfully, you will become a stronger, more effective, and satisfied student. Best of luck on your mastery of this Insider Language!

Insider Language Strategies

"See It, Say It!" Reading your Insider Language set aloud

"IT IS BETTER TO FAIL IN ORIGINALITY THAN TO SUCCEED IN IMITATION."
–HERMAN MELVILLE

Reading aloud is the foundation for the development of an Insider Language. It is the single most important thing you can do for vocabulary acquisition. Done correctly, it engages the visual, auditory, and speech centers of the brain and hastens its storage in your long-term memory.

Reading aloud demonstrates the relationship between the printed word and its meaning.

You can read aloud on a higher level than you can initially understand, so reading aloud makes complex ideas more accessible and exposes you to vocabulary and patterns that are not part of your typical speech. Reading aloud helps you understand the complicated text better and makes more challenging text easier to grasp and understand. Reading aloud helps you to develop the "habits of mind" the strongest students use.

Reading aloud will make connections to concepts in the reading that requires you to relate the new vocabulary to things you already know. Go to the glossary at the end of this book and for each word complete the five steps outlined below:

1. Read the word and its definition aloud. Focus on the sound of the word and how it looks on the paper.
2. Read the word aloud again try to say three or four similar words; this will help you build connections to closely related words.
3. Read the word aloud a third time. Try to make a connection to something you have read or heard.
4. Visualize the concept described in the term. Paint a mental picture of the word in use.
5. Try to think of the opposite of the word. Discovering a close antonym will help you place this word in context.

Create a sentence using the word in its proper context

"OPPORTUNITIES DON'T HAPPEN. YOU CREATE THEM." –CHRIS GROSSER

Context means the circumstances that form the setting for an event, statement, or idea, and which it can be fully understood and assessed. Synonyms for context include conditions, factors, situation, background, and setting.
Place the word in context by using it in a sentence. Write this sentence down and read it aloud. By creating sentences, you are practicing using the word correctly. If you strive to make these sentences interesting and creative, they will become more memorable and effective in activating your long-term memory.

Identify the Parts of Speech
"SUCCESS IS NOT FINAL; FAILURE IS NOT FATAL: IT IS THE COURAGE TO CONTINUE THAT COUNTS." –WINSTON S. CHURCHILL

Read through each term in the glossary and make a note of what part of speech each term is. Studying and identifying parts of speech shows us how the words relate to each other. It also helps you create a visualization of each term. Below are brief descriptions of the parts of speech for you to use as a guide.

VERB: A word denoting action, occurrence, or existence. Examples: walk, hop, whisper, sweat, dribbles, feels, sleeps, drink, smile, are, is, was, has.

NOUN: A word that names a person, place, thing, idea, animal, quality, or action. Nouns are the subject of the sentence. Examples: dog, Tom, Florida, CD, pasta, hate, tiger.

ADJECTIVE: A word that modifies, qualifies, or describes nouns and pronouns. Generally, adjectives appear immediately before the words they modify. Examples: smart girl, gifted teacher, old car, red door.

ADVERB: A word that modifies verbs, adjectives and other adverbs. An "ly" ending almost always changes an adjective to an adverb. Examples: ran swiftly, worked slowly, and drifted aimlessly. Many adverbs do not end in "ly." However, all adverbs identify when, where, how, how far, how much, etc. Examples: run hot, lived hard, moved right, study smart.

Chunking

"YOUR POSITIVE ACTION COMBINED WITH POSITIVE THINKING RESULTS IN SUCCESS." SHIV KHERA

Chunking is when you take a set of words and break it down into groups based on a common relationship. Research has shown that our brains learn by chunking information. By grouping your terms, you will be able to recall large sets of these words easily. To help make your chunking go easily use an online word cloud generator to make a set of word clouds representing your chunks.

1. Study the glossary and decide how you want to chunk the set of words. You can group by part of speech, topic, letter of the alphabet, word length, etc. Try to find an easy way to group each term.
2. Once you have your different groups, visit www.wordclouds.com to create a custom word cloud for each group. Print each one of these clouds and post it in a prominent place to serve as constant visual aids for your learning.

Analogies

"CHOOSE THE POSITIVE. YOU HAVE CHOICE, YOU ARE MASTER OF YOUR ATTITUDE, CHOOSE THE POSITIVE, THE CONSTRUCTIVE. OPTIMISM IS A FAITH THAT LEADS TO SUCCESS."– BRUCE LEE

An analogy is a comparison in which an idea or a thing is compared to another thing that is quite different from it. Analogies aim at explaining an idea by comparing it to something that is familiar. Metaphors and similes are tools used to create analogies.

Analogies are useful for learning vocabulary because they require you to analyze a word (or words), and then transfer that analysis to another word. This transfer reinforces the understanding of all the words.

As you analyze the relationships between the analogies you are creating, you will begin to understand the complex relationships between the seemingly unrelated words.

__A__ is to __B__ as __C__ is to __D__

This can be written using colons in place of the terms "is to" and "as."

A:B::C:D

The two items on the left (items A & B) describe a relationship and are separated by a single colon. The two items on the right (items C & D) are shown on the right and are also separated by a colon. Together, both sides are then separated by two colons in the middle, as shown here: Tall: Short :: Skinny: Fat. The relationship used in this analogy is the antonym.

How to create an analogy

Start with the basic formula for an analogy:

_____ : _____ :: _____ : _____

Next, we will examine a simple synonym analogy:

automobile : car :: box : crate

The key to figuring out a set of word analogies is determining the relationship between the paired set of words.

Here is a list of the most common types of Analogies and examples

Synonym	Scream : Yell :: Push : Shove
Antonym	Rich : Poor :: Empty : Full
Cause is to Effect	Prosperity : Happiness :: Success : Joy
A Part is to its Whole	Toe : Foot :: Piece : Set
An Object to its Function	Car : Travel :: Read : Learn
A Item is to its Category	Tabby : House Cat :: Doberman : Dog
Word is a symptom of the other	Pain : Fracture :: Wheezing : Allergy
An object and it's description	Glass : Brittle :: Lead : Dense
The word is lacking the second word	Amputee : Limb :: Deaf : Hearing
The first word Hinders the second word	Shackles : Movement :: Stagger : Walk
The first word helps the action of the second	Knife : Bread :: Screwdriver : Screw
This word is made up of the second word	Sweater : Wool :: Jeans : Denim
A word and it's definition	Cede: Break Away :: Abolish : To get rid of

Using words from the glossary, make a set of analogies using each one. As a bonus, use more than one glossary term in a single analogy.

_____ : _____ :: _____ : _____

Name the relationship between the words in your analogy:_____

_____ : _____ :: _____ : _____

Name the relationship between the words in your analogy:_____

_____ : _____ :: _____ : _____

Name the relationship between the words in your analogy:_____

Mnemonics

"IT ISN'T THE MOUNTAINS AHEAD TO CLIMB THAT WEAR YOU OUT; IT'S THE PEBBLE IN YOUR SHOE."   –MUHAMMAD ALI

A mnemonic is a learning technique that helps you retain and remember information. Mnemonics are one of the best learning methods for remembering lists or processes in order. Mnemonics make the material more meaningful by adding associations and creating patterns. Interestingly, mnemonics may work better when they utilize absurd, startling, or shocking examples and references. Mnemonics help organize the information so that you can easily retrieve it later. By giving you associations and cues, mnemonics allow you to form a mental structure ordering a list or process to help you remember it better. This mental structure allows you to create a structure of association between items that may not appear to have any relationship. Mnemonics typically use references that are easy to visualize and thus easier to remember. Through visualization of vivid images and references, the information is much easier to imprint into long-term memory. The power of making mnemonics lies in converting dull, inert and uninspiring information into something vibrant and memorable.

How to make simple and effective mnemonics
Some of the best mnemonics help us remember simple rules or lists in order.

Step 1. Take a list of terms you are trying to remember in order. For example, we will use the scientific method:

observation, question, hypothesis, methods, results, and conclusion.

Next, we will replace each word on the list with a new word that starts with the same letter. These new words will together form a vivid sentence that is easy to remember:

Objectionable Queens Haunted Macho Rednecks Creatively.

As silly as the above sentence seems, it is easy to remember, and now we can call on this sentence to remind us of the order of the scientific method.

Visit http://www.mnemonicgenerator.com/ and try typing in a list of words. It is fun to see the mnemonics that it makes and shows how easy it is to make great mnemonics to help your studying.

Using vivid words in your mnemonics allows you to see the sentence you are making. Words that are gross, scary, or name interesting animals are helpful. Profanity is also useful because the shock value can trigger memory. The following are lists of vivid words to use in your mnemonics:

Gross words

Moist, Gurgle, Phlegm, Fetus, Curd, Smear, Squirt, Chunky, Orifice, Maggots, Viscous, Queasy, Bulbous, Pustule, Putrid, Fester, Secrete, Munch, Vomit, Ooze, Dripping, Roaches, Mucus, Stink, Stank, Stunk, Slurp, Pus, Lick, Salty, Tongue, Fart, Flatulence, Hemorrhoid.

Interesting Animals

Aardvark, Baboon, Chicken, Chinchilla, Duck, Dragonfly, Emu, Electric Eel, Frog, Flamingo, Gecko, Hedgehog, Hyena, Iguana, Jackal, Jaguar, Leopard, Lynx, Minnow, Manatee, Mongoose, Neanderthal, Newt, Octopus, Oyster, Pelican, Penguin, Platypus, Quail, Racoon, Rattlesnake, Rhinoceros, Scorpion, Seahorse, Toucan, Turkey, Vulture, Weasel, Woodpecker, Yak, Zebra.

Superhero Words

Diabolical, Activate, Boom, Clutch, Dastardly, Dynamic, Dynamite, Shazam, Kaboom, Zip, Zap, Zoom, Zany, Crushing, Smashing, Exploding, Ripping, Tearing.

Scary Words

Apparition, Bat, Chill, Demon, Eerie, Fangs, Genie, Hell, Lantern, Macabre, Nightmare, Owl, Ogre, Phantasm, Repulsive, Scarecrow, Tarantula, Undead, Vampire, Wraith, Zombie.

There are several types of mnemonics that can help your memory.

1. Images

Visual mnemonics are a type of mnemonic that works by associating an image with characters or objects whose name sounds like the item that must be memorized. This is one of the easiest ways to create effective mnemonics. An example would be to use the shape of numbers to help memorize a long list of them. Numbers can be memorized by their shapes, so that: 0 -looks like an egg; 1 -a pencil, or a candle; 2 -a snake; 3 -an ear; 4 -a sailboat; 5 -a key; 6 -a comet; 7 -a knee; 8 -a snowman; 9 -a comma.

Another type of visual mnemonic is the word-length mnemonic in which the number of letters in each word corresponds to a digit. This simple mnemonic gives pi to seven decimal places:

3.141582 becomes "How I wish I could calculate pi."

Of course, you could use this type of mnemonic to create a longer sentence showing the digits of an important number. Some people have used this type of mnemonic to memorize thousands of digits.

Using the hands is also an important tool for creating visual objects. Making the hands into specific shapes can help us remember the pattern of things or the order of a list of things.

2. Rhyming

Rhyming mnemonics are quick ways to make things memorable. A classic example is a mnemonic for the number of days in each month:
"30 days hath September, April, June, and November.
All the rest have 31
Except February, my dear son.
It has 28, and that is fine
But in Leap Year it has 29."

Another example of a rhyming mnemonic is a common spelling rule:
"I before e except after c
or when sounding like a
in neighbor and weigh."

Use **rhymer.com** to get large lists of rhyming words.

3. Homonym

A homonym is one of a group of words that share the same pronunciation but have different meanings, whether spelled the same or not.

Try saying what you're attempting to remember out loud or very quickly, and see if anything leaps out. If you know other languages, using similar-sounding words from those can be effective.

You could also browse this list of homonyms
at http://www.cooper.com/alan/homonym_list.html.

4. Onomatopoeia

An Onomatopeia is a word that phonetically imitates, resembles or suggests the source of the sound that it describes. Are there any noises made by the thing you're trying to memorize? Is it often associated with some other sound? Failing that, just make up a noise that seems to fit.

Achoo, ahem, baa, bam, bark, beep, beep beep, belch, bleat, boo, boo hoo, boom, burp, buzz, chirp, click clack, crash, croak, crunch, cuckoo, dash, drip, ding dong, eek, fizz, flit, flutter, gasp, grrr, ha ha, hee hee, hiccup, hiss, hissing, honk, icky, itchy, jiggly, jangle, knock knock, lush, la la la, mash, meow, moan, murmur, neigh, oink, ouch, plop, pow, quack, quick, rapping, rattle, ribbit, roar, rumble, rustle, scratch, sizzle, skittering, snap crackle pop, splash, splish splash, spurt, swish, swoosh, tap, tapping, tick tock, tinkle, tweet, ugh, vroom, wham, whinny, whip, whooping, woof.

5. Acronyms

An acronym is a word or name formed as an abbreviation from the initial components of a word, such as NATO, which stands for North Atlantic Treaty Organization. If you're trying to memorize something involving letters, this is often a good bet. A lot of famous mnemonics are acronyms, such as ROYGBIV which stands for the order of colors in the light spectrum (Red, Orange, Yellow, Green, Blue, Indigo, and Violet).

A great acronym generator to try is: www.all-acronyms.com.

A different spin on an acronym is a backronym. A **backronym** is a specially constructed phrase that is supposed to be the source of a word that is an acronym. A backronym is constructed by creating a new phrase to fit an already existing word, name, or acronym.

The word is a combination of *backward* and *acronym*, and has been defined as a "reverse acronym." For example, the United States Department of Justice assigns to their Amber Alert program the meaning "**A**merica's **M**issing: **B**roadcast **E**mergency **R**esponse." The process can go either way to make good mnemonics.

Visit: https://arthurdick.com/projects/backronym/ to try out a simple backronym generator.

6. Anagrams

An anagram is a direct word switch or word play, the result of rearranging the letters of a word or phrase to produce a new word or phrase, using all the original letters exactly once; for example, the word anagram can be rearranged into nag-a-ram.

Try re-arranging letters or components and see if anything memorable emerges. Visit http://www.nameacronym.net/ to use a simple anagram generator.

One particularly memorable form of anagram is the spoonerism, where you swap the initial syllables or letters of words to make new phrases. These are usually humorous, and this makes them easier to remember. Here are some examples:

"Is it kisstomary to cuss the bride?" (as opposed to "customary to kiss")
"The Lord is a shoving leopard." (instead of "a loving shepherd")
"A blushing crow." ("crushing blow")
"A well-boiled icicle" ("well-oiled bicycle")
"You were fighting a liar in the quadrangle." ("lighting a fire")
"Is the bean dizzy?" (as opposed to "is the dean busy?")

7. Stories

Make up quick stories or incidents involving the material you want to memorize. For larger chunks of information, the stories can get more elaborate. Structured stories are particularly good for remembering lists or other sequenced information. Have a look at https://en.wikipedia.org/wiki/Method_of_loci for a more advanced memory sequencing technique.

Visual Metaphors

"LIMITS, LIKE FEAR, IS OFTEN AN ILLUSION." –MICHAEL JORDAN

What is a Metaphor?

A metaphor is a figure of speech that refers to one thing by mentioning another thing. Metaphors provide clarity and identify hidden similarities between two seemingly unrelated ideas. A visual metaphor is an image that creates a link between different ideas.

Visual metaphors help us use our understanding of the world to learn new concepts, skills, and ideas. Visual metaphors help us relate new material to what we already know. Visual metaphors must be clear and simple enough to spark a connection and understanding. Visual metaphors should use familiar things to help you be less fearful of new, complex, or challenging topics. Metaphors trigger a sense of familiarity so that you are more accepting of the new idea. Metaphors work best when you associate a familiar, easy to understand idea with a challenging, obscure, or abstract concept.

How to make a visual metaphor

1. Brainstorm using the words of the concept. Use different fonts, colors, or shapes to represent parts of the concept.

2. Merge these images together

3. Show the process using arrows, accents, etc.

4. Think about the story line your metaphor projects.

Examples of visual metaphors:

A skeleton used to show a framework of something.

A cloud showing an outline.

A bodybuilder whose muscles represent supporting ideas and details.

A sandwich where the meat, tomato, and lettuce represent supporting ideas.

A recipe card to show a process.

Your metaphor should be accurate. It should be complex enough to convey meaning, but simple and clear enough to be easily understood.

Morphology
"SCIENCE IS THE CAPTAIN, AND PRACTICE THE SOLDIERS." LEONARDO DA VINCI

Morphology is the study of the origin, roots, suffixes, and prefixes of the words. Understanding the meaning of prefixes, suffixes, and roots make it easier to decode the meaning of new vocabulary. Having the ability to decode using morphology increases text comprehension when initially reading as well.

The capability of identifying meaningful parts of words (morphemes), including prefixes, suffixes, and roots can be helpful. Identifying morphemes improves decoding accuracy and fluency. Reading speed improves when you can decode larger chunks of text quickly. When you can recognize morphemes in words, you will be better able to make sense of new words in context. Below are charts containing the most common prefixes, suffixes, and root words. Use them to help you decode your vocabulary terms.

Prefixes

Prefix	Meaning	Example words and meanings	
a, ab, abs	away from	absent abdicate	not to be present, to give up an office or throne.
ad, a, ac, af, ag, an, ar, at, as	to, toward	Advance advantage	To move forward To have the upper hand
anti	against	Antidote antisocial antibiotic	To repair poisoning refers to someone who's not social
bi, bis	two	bicycle binary biweekly	two-wheeled cycle two number system every two weeks
circum, cir	around	circumnavigate circle	Travel around the world a figure that goes all around
com, con, co, col	with, together	Complete Complement	To finish To go along with
de	away from, down, the opposite of	depart detour	to go away from to go out of your way
dis, dif, di	apart	dislike dishonest distant	not to like not honest away
En-, em-	Cause to	Entrance	the way in.
epi	upon, on top of	epitaph epilogue epidemic	writing upon a tombstone speech at the end, on top of the rest
equ, equi	equal	equalize equitable	to make equal fair, equal
ex, e, ef	out, from	exit eject exhale	to go out to throw out to breathe out
Fore-	Before	Forewarned	To have prior warning

Prefix	Meaning	Example Words and Meanings	
in, il, ir, im, en	in, into	Infield Imbibe	The inner playing field to take part in
in, il, ig, ir, im	not	inactive ignorant irreversible irritate	not active not knowing not reversible to put into discomfort
inter	between, among	international interact	among nations to mix with
mal, male	bad, ill, wrong	malpractice malfunction	bad practice fail to function, bad function
Mid	Middle	Amidships	In the middle of a ship
mis	wrong, badly	misnomer	The wrong name
mono	one, alone, single	monocle	one lensed glasses
non	not, the reverse of	nonprofit	not making a profit
ob	in front, against, in front of, in the way of	Obsolete	No longer needed
omni	everywhere, all	omnipresent omnipotent	always present, everywhere all powerful
Over	On top	Overdose	Take too much medication
Pre	Before	Preview	Happens before a show.
per	through	Permeable pervasive	to pass through, all encompassing
poly	many	Polygamy polygon	many spouses figure with many sides
post	after	postpone postmortem	to do after after death
pre	before, earlier than	Predict Preview	To know before To view before release
pro	forward, going ahead of, supporting	proceed pro-war promote	to go forward supporting the war to raise or move forward
re	again, back	retell recall reverse	to tell again to call back to go back
se	apart	secede seclude	to withdraw, become apart to stay apart from others
Semi	Half	Semipermeable	Half-permeable

Prefix	Meaning	Example Words and Meanings	
Sub	under, less than	Submarine	under water
super	over, above, greater	superstar superimpose	a start greater than her stars to put over something else
trans	across	transcontinental transverse	across the continent to lie or go across
un, uni	one	unidirectional unanimous unilateral	having one direction sharing one view having one side
un	not	uninterested unhelpful unethical	not interested not helpful not ethical

Roots

Root	Meaning	Example words & meanings	
act, ag	to do, to act	Agent Activity	One who acts as a representative Action
Aqua	Water	Aquamarine	The color of water
Aud	To hear	Auditorium	A place to hear music
apert	open	Aperture	An opening
bas	low	Basement Basement	Something that is low, at the bottom A room that is low
Bio	Living thing	Biological	Living matter
cap, capt, cip, cept, ceive	to take, to hold, to seize	Captive Receive Capable Recipient	One who is held To take Able to take hold of things One who takes hold or receives
ced, cede, ceed, cess	to go, to give in	Precede Access Proceed	To go before Means of going to To go forward
Cogn	Know	Cognitive	Ability to think
cred, credit	to believe	Credible Incredible Credit	Believable Not believable Belief, trust
curr, curs, cours	to run	Current Precursory Recourse	Now in progress, running Running (going) before To run for aid
Cycle	Circle	Lifecycle	The circle of life
dic, dict	to say	Dictionary Indict	A book explaining words (sayings)

Root	Meaning	Examples and meanings	
duc, duct	to lead	Induce	To lead to action
		Conduct	To lead or guide
		Aqueduct	Pipe that leads water somewhere
equ	equal, even	Equality	Equal in social, political rights
		Equanimity	Evenness of mind, tranquility
fac, fact, fic, fect, fy	to make, to do	Facile	Easy to do
		Fiction	Something that is made up
		Factory	Place that makes things
		Affect	To make a change in
fer, ferr	to carry, bring	Defer	To carry away
		Referral	Bring a source for help/information
Gen	Birth	Generate	To create something
graph	write	Monograph	A writing on a particular subject
		Graphite	A form of carbon used for writing
Loc	Place	Location	A place
Mater	Mother	Maternity	Expecting birth
Mem	Recall	Memory	The recall experiences
mit, mis	to send	Admit	To send in
		Missile	Something sent through the air
Nat	Born	Native	Born in a place
par	equal	Parity	Equality
		Disparate	No equal, not alike
Ped	Foot	Podiatrist	Foot doctor
Photo	Light	Photograph	A picture
plic	to fold, to bend, to turn	Complicate	To fold (mix) together
		Implicate	To fold in, to involve
pon, pos, posit, pose	to place	Component	A part placed together with others
		Transpose	A place across
		Compose	To put many parts into place
		Deposit	To place for safekeeping
scrib, script	to write	Describe	To write about or tell about
		Transcript	A written copy
		Subscription	A written signature or document
sequ, secu	to follow	Sequence	In following order

Root	Meaning	Examples and Meanings	
Sign	Mark	Signal	to alert somebody
spec, spect, spic	to appear, to look, to see	Specimen Aspect	An example to look at One way to see something
sta, stat, sist,	to stand, or make stand	Constant	Standing with
stit, sisto	Stable, steady	Status Stable Desist	Social standing Steady (standing) To stand away from
Struct	To build	Construction	To build a thing
tact	to touch	Contact Tactile	To touch together To be able to be touched
ten, tent, tain	to hold	Tenable Retentive Maintain	Able to be held, holding Holding To keep or hold up
tend, tens, tent	to stretch	Extend Tension	To stretch or draw out Stretched
Therm	Temperature	Thermometer	Detects temperature
tract	to draw	Attract Contract	To draw together An agreement drawn up
ven, vent	to come	Convene Advent	To come together A coming
Vis	See	Invisible	Cannot be seen
ver, vert, vers	to turn	Avert Revert Reverse	To turn away To turn back To turn around

Crossword Puzzles

1. Using the Across and Down clues, write the correct words in the numbered grid below.

ACROSS

2. Valve actuated by magnetic action by means of an electrically energized coil.
6. A substance formed by a union of two or more elements
9. Evaporates low pressure vapor from the expansion device
11. A mixture of at least two different liquids.
14. An AC motor which operates on principle of rotating magnetic field. Rotor has no electrical connection, but receives electrical energy by transformer action from field windings.
16. Converting recycled refrigerant into a product to be reused.
17. A passive throttling device, comprised of a small opening, located upstream of the evaporator.
18. High-efficiency design motor used on virtually all of today's HVAC & R equipment requiring motors.
19. Any material or substance which has the ability to retard the flow or transfer of heat.
20. Change in temperature of a gas on expansion through a porous plug from a high pressure to a lower pressure.

DOWN

1. Special high efficiency device (pump) used create deep vacuum within an AC
3. A unit of Pressure equal to exactly 760 mmHg
4. Reduction in pressure below atmospheric pressure.
5. Device used to electrically shut down a refrigerating unit when unsafe pressures and
7. An independent refrigeration system that separates the non-condensables from the refrigerant and re-condenses and collects any refrigerant in the exhaust vent stream.
8. The rate at which an appliance is losing refrigerant.
10. Gas phase
11. Any device which contains a refrigerant and which is used for household or commercial purposes, including any air conditioner, refrigerator, chiller, or freezer.
12. Unit of electrical power.
13. The total amount of moisture in air.
15. To extract refrigerant from an appliance and clean refrigerant for reuse without meeting all of the requirements for reclamation.

A. Orifice Plate
B. Recycle
C. Solenoid Valve
D. Vacuum
E. Insulation
F. Induction Motor
G. Joule
H. Watt
I. Leak Rate
J. Azeotroph
K. Vacuum Pump
L. Safety Control
M. Reclaim
N. Evaporator
O. Appliance
P. Purge unit
Q. Compound
R. Atmosphere
S. Humidity
T. Vapor
U. PSC Motor

2. Using the Across and Down clues, write the correct words in the numbered grid below.

ACROSS

5. Connects manifold to recovery device.
7. In some air conditioning systems, vacuum is used to operate dampers and controls in system.
9. A standard unit of measure for electrical resistance.
12. Forming a homogeneous mixture of liquids when added together.
13. The fluid used for heat transfer in a refrigeration system, which absorbs heat during evaporation at low temperature and pressure, and releases heat during condensation.
16. Pressure or temperature settings of a control; change within limits.
17. Volume displaced by piston as it travels length of stroke.
18. The Pressure exerted by a particular Gas in a mixture.
19. An AC motor which operates on principle of rotating magnetic field. Rotor has no electrical connection, but receives electrical energy by transformer action from field windings.

DOWN

1. Unit of electrical capacity; capacity of a condenser which, when charged with one coulomb of electricity, gives difference of potential of one volt.
2. A refrigerant has a boiling point below minus 50C or minus 58F at atmospheric pressure.
3. A unit of Pressure equal to exactly 760 mmHg
4. The rate at which an appliance is losing refrigerant.
6. The heart or "pump" within an air conditioning or heat pump system.
8. To determine; position indicators as required to obtain accurate measurements.
10. Group of electrical terminals housed in protective box or container.
11. Reducing contaminants in the used refrigerant
14. To remove water from a system.
15. The force exerted per unit area of surface.
16. Converting recycled refrigerant into a product to be reused.

A. Atmosphere
D. Dehydrate
G. Vacuum Control System
J. Refrigerant
M. Pressure
P. Calibrate
S. Recycle

B. Induction Motor
E. Leak Rate
H. Piston Displacement
K. Very high pressure
N. Range
Q. Miscible
T. Farad

C. OHM
F. Partial Pressure
I. Compressor
L. Center port
O. Junction Box
R. Reclaim

25

3. Using the Across and Down clues, write the correct words in the numbered grid below.

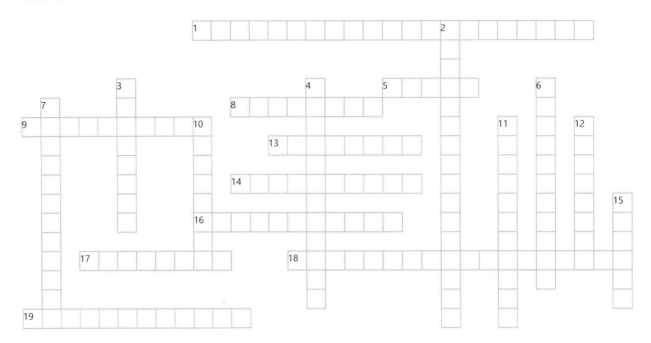

ACROSS

1. Need to evacuate system to eliminate air and moisture at the end of service.
5. Gas phase
8. Receives high pressure liquid from the condenser
9. Special high efficiency device (pump) used create deep vacuum within an AC
13. Gas used for leak detection.
14. States that the volume occupied by a gas at a constant Pressure is directly proportional to the absolute temperature.
16. Degree of hotness or coldness as measured by a thermometer
17. The force exerted per unit area of surface.
18. Volume displaced by piston as it travels length of stroke.
19. Pressure which exists in condensing side of refrigerating system.

DOWN

2. Gauge pressure plus atmospheric pressure (14.7 lbs. per sq. in.).
3. The total amount of moisture in air.
4. The action of purifying a liquid by a process of heating and cooling.
6. Substance used to counteract acids, in refrigeration system.
7. Pressure in low side of refrigerating system; also called suction pressure or low side pressure.
10. High-efficiency design motor used on virtually all of today's HVAC & R equipment requiring motors.
11. Self piercing valve body designed to be permanently silver brazed or clamped to refrigerant tubing surface.
12. That time period of a refrigeration cycle when the system is not operating.
15. Device for removing small particles from a fluid.

A. Filter
D. Head Pressure
G. Vapor
J. Neutralizer
M. Nitrogen
P. Off Cycle
S. Receiver

B. Vacuum Pump
E. Saddle Valve
H. Back Pressure
K. Distillation
N. Dehydration Evacuation
Q. Humidity

C. Absolute Pressure
F. Pressure
I. Charles Law
L. Temperature
O. PSC Motor
R. Piston Displacement

4. Using the Across and Down clues, write the correct words in the numbered grid below.

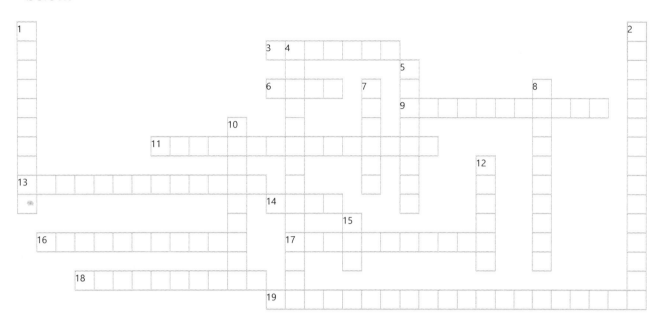

ACROSS

3. Unit used for measuring relative loudness of sounds.
6. Unit of electrical power.
9. Self piercing valve body designed to be permanently silver brazed or clamped to refrigerant tubing surface.
11. Requires the assistance of components such as the appliance or unit's compressor to remove the refrigerant from the appliance.
13. Condition in which refrigerant and
14. Electrical "pressure" applied to a circuit.
16. A substance produces a refrigerating or cooling effect while expanding or vaporizing.
17. Property of non-conductor that permits storage of electrical energy in an electrostatic field.
18. A unit of Pressure equal to exactly 760 mmHg
19. Breaks down the CFCs and frees the chlorine ion at stratosphere.

DOWN

1. Heat energy absorbed in process of changing form of substance without change in temperature or pressure.
2. Specially processed carbon used as a filter drier; commonly used to clean air.
4. Where heat is absorbed by warm air passing across. Liquid refrigerant boils as it is metered into coil, and changes from liquid to vapor.
5. A solution or surface that is capable of soaking up (taking in) another substance or energy form.
7. The SI base unit of temperature; a unit on an absolute temperature scale.
8. Special high efficiency device (pump) used create deep vacuum within an AC
10. Unit of electrical power, equal to 1000 watts.
12. One of a group of substances having the same combination of elements but arranged spatially in different ways.
15. A radial or axial flow device used for moving or producing artificial currents of air.

A. Saddle Valve	B. Fan	C. Watt	D. Passive recovery
E. Kilometer	F. Evaporator Coil	G. Acid Condition	H. Decibel
I. Refrigerant	J. Ultraviolet Radiation	K. Atmosphere	L. Isomer
M. Latent Heat	N. Absorber	O. Capacitance	P. Activated Carbon
Q. Vacuum Pump	R. Volt	S. Kelvin	

5. Using the Across and Down clues, write the correct words in the numbered grid below.

ACROSS

1. Type of torch used to detect halogen refrigerant leaks.
6. A chemical used in fire extinguishing.
8. Any products that are fully manufactured, charged, and hermetically sealed in a factory with five pounds or less of refrigerant
11. A radial or axial flow device used for moving or producing artificial currents of air.
12. Receives high pressure liquid from the condenser
13. Latin for the least amount of Refrigerant you can release into the atmosphere.
14. Evaporates low pressure vapor from the expansion device
15. Round or rectangular pipes or controlled paths acting as conduit for return, mixed, makeup, supply or exhaust air.
16. The process of collecting used refrigerant.
17. Process whereas additional sensible heat (as opposed to latent heat) is removed from condensed refrigerant liquid prior to the metering device.
19. Fluid opening

DOWN

2. A substance formed by a union of two or more elements
3. A combination shut-off and service value typically used on the inlet and outlet of a compressor.
4. To determine; position indicators as required to obtain accurate measurements.
5. Valve for controlling airflow. Found in duct work, movable plate opens and closes to control airflow.
7. Tool which is principally a torch and when an air refrigerant mixture is fed to flame, this flame will change color in presence of heated copper.
9. The process of extracting any air, non-condensable gases, or water from the system.
10. A unit of measurement used for determining cooling capacity. One ton is the equivalent of 12,000 BTUs per hour.
18. Vapor phase or state of a substance.

A. Flame Test   B. De Minimus   C. Sub Cooling   D. Calibrate
E. Ductwork   F. Damper   G. Small appliance   H. Halide Torch
I. Evacuation   J. Evaporator   K. Fan   L. Halon
M. Compound   N. Recovery   O. Receiver   P. King Valve
Q. TON   R. Gas   S. Back Seating

6. Using the Across and Down clues, write the correct words in the numbered grid below.

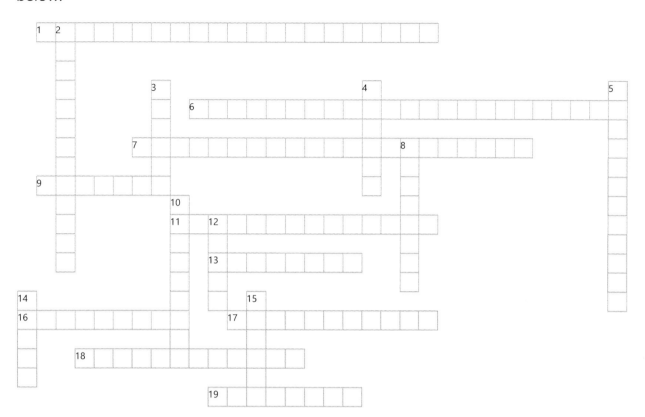

ACROSS

1. The temperature where a refrigerant exists in both liquid and vapor form relative to its measured pressure.
6. Temperature at which molecular motion ceases.
7. Need to evacuate system to eliminate air and moisture at the end of service.
9. A blend of two or more components that do not a have fixed proportion to one another.
11. Equipment that has its own compressor or pump.
13. The process in which a gas flows through a small hole in a container.
16. Substance with ability to take up, or absorb another substance.
17. Instrument used to measure pressures below atmospheric pressure.
18. A refrigerant has a boiling point between minus 50C and 10C degrees at atmospheric pressure.
19. The total amount of moisture in air.

DOWN

2. Condition in which refrigerant and
3. Unit of measure referring to the flow of electrons within a circuit.
4. The SI base unit of temperature; a unit on an absolute temperature scale.
5. Pressure which exists in condensing side of refrigerating system.
8. The atom found in CFC and HCFC refrigerants that destroys ozone in the stratosphere.
10. Instrument to measuring pressure of gases and vapors.
12. Quantity of heat equivalent to 100,000 Btu.
14. The Gaseous state of any kind of matter that normally exists as a liquid or solid.
15. Reduction in pressure below atmospheric pressure.

A. Head Pressure
D. Vacuum
G. Therm
J. Humidity
M. Manometer
P. Active recovery
S. Saturation Temperature

B. Mixture
E. Absolute Zero Temperature
H. Acid Condition
K. Vapor
N. Vacuum Gauge
Q. Kelvin

C. Ampere
F. Chlorine
I. Dehydration Evacuation
L. Absorbent
O. Effusion
R. High pressure

7. Using the Across and Down clues, write the correct words in the numbered grid below.

ACROSS

2. Electrical resistance mounted in or around liquid receiver, used to maintain head pressures when ambient temperature is at freezing or below freezing.
5. Device which releases the contents of a container above normal pressures, and before rupture pressures are reached.
11. Evaporates low pressure vapor from the expansion device
12. Device used to measure quantities of heat or determine specific heats.
13. Connects manifold to recovery device.
14. Converts high pressure liquid to low pressure vapor
15. Fluid opening
16. Accumulates any low pressure liquid from the evaporator so it can vaporize before entering the compressor
17. High-efficiency design motor used on virtually all of today's HVAC & R equipment requiring motors.
18. Chemical used as a drier or desiccant.

DOWN

1. Equipment that has its own compressor or pump.
2. The parts of an appliance that are normally connected to each other and are designed to contain refrigerant.
3. Where heat is absorbed by warm air passing across. Liquid refrigerant boils as it is metered into coil, and changes from liquid to vapor.
4. Gray cylinder with a yellow top; used for recovery or transporting refrigerant.
6. A form of testing for high pressure cylinders.
7. A device equipped with gauges and manual valves, used by serviceman to service refrigerating systems.
8. Measures low pressure and vacuum.
9. Specially processed carbon used as a filter drier; commonly used to clean air.
10. A refrigerant has a boiling point above 10C or 50F at atmospheric pressure.

A. Compound gauge
D. Calorimeter
G. Receiver Heating Element
J. Evaporator
M. Reusable cylinders
P. Accumulator
S. PSC Motor

B. Refrigerant circuit
E. Center port
H. Active recovery
K. Activated Carbon
N. Activated Alumina
Q. Service Manifold

C. Evaporator Coil
F. Hydrostatic
I. Back Seating
L. Safety Plug
O. Low pressure
R. Expansion device

30

8. Using the Across and Down clues, write the correct words in the numbered grid below.

ACROSS

1. Family of refrigerants containing halogen chemicals.
3. Induced currents flowing in a core.
5. A combination shut-off and service value typically used on the inlet and outlet of a compressor.
7. Forming a homogeneous mixture of liquids when added together.
11. Chemical compound which is used as a drying agent or desiccant in liquid line filter dryers.
14. Represents the amount of energy required to raise one pound of water one degree Fahrenheit.
16. An independent refrigeration system that separates the non-condensables from the refrigerant and re-condenses and collects any refrigerant in the exhaust vent stream.
17. Gas phase
18. Low pressure
19. Unit of electrical capacity; capacity of a condenser which, when charged with one coulomb of electricity, gives difference of potential of one volt.

DOWN

2. A mixture of at least two different liquids.
4. The difference between the Dew Point and the Bubble Point.
6. In flowing fluid, height of fluid equivalent to its velocity pressure.
8. Special high efficiency device (pump) used create deep vacuum within an AC
9. Group of electrical terminals housed in protective box or container.
10. Each refrigerant in the blend keeps its own temperature and pressure characteristics.
12. Close fitting part which moves up and down in a cylinder.
13. Side by side and having the same distance continuously between them.
15. Invisible, odorless, and tasteless mixture of gases which form earth's atmosphere.

A. Purge unit	B. Miscible	C. Farad	D. Junction Box
E. Blue	F. Temperature Glide	G. Vapor	H. Velocity Head
I. Zeotropic	J. Halide Refrigerants	K. Eddy Currents	L. Air
M. Vacuum Pump	N. Azeotroph	O. King Valve	P. British Thermal Unit
Q. Calcium Sulfate	R. Parallel	S. Piston	

9. Using the Across and Down clues, write the correct words in the numbered grid below.

ACROSS

1. Need to evacuate system to eliminate air and moisture at the end of service.
3. Special high efficiency device (pump) used create deep vacuum within an AC
7. Where heat is absorbed by warm air passing across. Liquid refrigerant boils as it is metered into coil, and changes from liquid to vapor.
12. Single use cylinders. Empty cylinders should have the pressure reduced to zero and the cylinder rendered unusable.
14. Heat energy absorbed in process of changing form of substance without change in temperature or pressure.
15. Low pressure
16. Device or instrument such as a halide torch, an electronic sniffer; or soap solution used to detect leaks.
17. In flowing fluid, height of fluid equivalent to its velocity pressure.
18. The temperature at which the non-azeotropic blend first begins to condense.
19. The piping used to connect the outdoor unit to the indoor unit.

DOWN

2. Converting recycled refrigerant into a product to be reused.
4. One thousandth of a millimeter.
5. An independent refrigeration system that separates the non-condensables from the refrigerant and re-condenses and collects any refrigerant in the exhaust vent stream.
6. A separation process in which a certain quantity of a mixture is divided during a phase transition
8. Typically, a multi ported valve used by service technicians to isolate remote system components, as well as check pressures and charge refrigerating units.
9. Connects manifold to recovery device.
10. An instrument for measuring resistance in ohms.
11. Evaporates low pressure vapor from the expansion device
13. The process in which a gas flows through a small hole in a container.

A. Center port
D. Evaporator
G. Reclaim
J. Leak Detector
M. Fractionation
P. Ohmmeter
S. Velocity Head

B. Dew Point
E. Purge unit
H. Line Set
K. Effusion
N. Latent Heat
Q. Service Valve

C. Vacuum Pump
F. Disposable cylinders
I. Evaporator Coil
L. Blue
O. Micron
R. Dehydration Evacuation

10. Using the Across and Down clues, write the correct words in the numbered grid below.

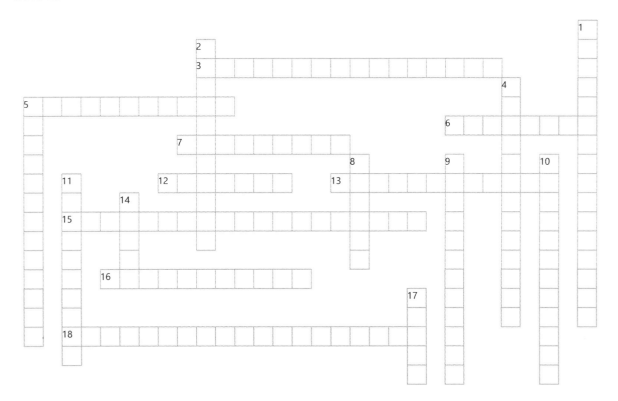

ACROSS

3. Amount of moisture in the air, indicated in grains per cubic foot.
5. Storage tank which receives liquid refrigerant from evaporator and prevents it from flowing into suction line.
6. An instrument for measuring resistance in ohms.
7. The process whereby a gas spreads out through another gas to occupy the space with uniform partial Pressure.
12. Any maintenance or repair on an appliance that would release refrigerant from the appliance to the atmosphere.
13. A refrigerant has a boiling point between minus 50C and 10C degrees at atmospheric pressure.
15. A temperature scale in which the lowest temperature that can be attained theoretically is zero
16. Degree of hotness or coldness as measured by a thermometer
18. Temperature measured from absolute zero.

DOWN

1. The difference between the Dew Point and the Bubble Point.
2. Device used to measure quantities of heat or determine specific heats.
4. Measures low pressure and vacuum.
5. Condition in which refrigerant and
8. Device for removing small particles from a fluid.
9. Pressure which exists in condensing side of refrigerating system.
10. Typically, a multi ported valve used by service technicians to isolate remote system components, as well as check pressures and charge refrigerating units.
11. Pressure of fluid expressed in terms of height of column of the fluid, such as water or mercury.
14. Change in temperature of a gas on expansion through a porous plug from a high pressure to a lower pressure.
17. Quantity of heat equivalent to 100,000 Btu.

A. Absolute Temperature
D. Absolute Temperature
G. Acid Condition
J. Diffusion
M. Head Pressure
P. Calorimeter
S. High pressure

B. Temperature Glide
E. Filter
H. Service Valve
K. Accumulator
N. Compound gauge
Q. Static Head

C. Absolute Humidity
F. Therm
I. Temperature
L. Joule
O. Opening
R. Ohmmeter

11. Using the Across and Down clues, write the correct words in the numbered grid below.

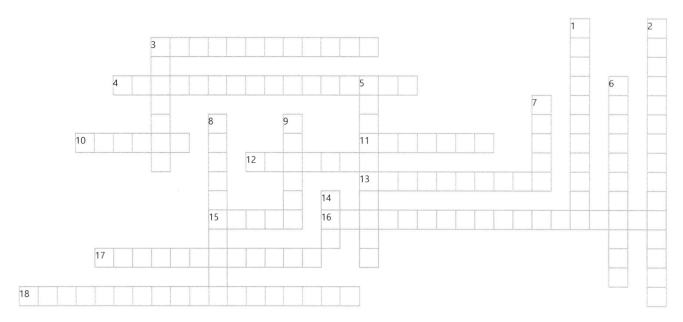

ACROSS

3. Device or instrument such as a halide torch, an electronic sniffer; or soap solution used to detect leaks.
4. Treaty among nations designed to protect the stratospheric ozone layer.
10. Valve for controlling airflow. Found in duct work, movable plate opens and closes to control airflow.
11. Converting recycled refrigerant into a product to be reused.
12. Unit used for measuring relative loudness of sounds.
13. Evaporates low pressure vapor from the expansion device
15. Quantity of heat equivalent to 100,000 Btu.
16. Family of refrigerants containing halogen chemicals.
17. A refrigerant has a boiling point between minus 50C and 10C degrees at atmospheric pressure.
18. The parts of an appliance that are normally connected to each other and are designed to contain refrigerant.

DOWN

1. Storage tank which receives liquid refrigerant from evaporator and prevents it from flowing into suction line.
2. The Pressure exerted by a particular Gas in a mixture.
3. The piping used to connect the outdoor unit to the indoor unit.
5. States that the volume occupied by a gas at a constant Pressure is directly proportional to the absolute temperature.
6. Group of electrical terminals housed in protective box or container.
7. The Gaseous state of any kind of matter that normally exists as a liquid or solid.
8. Heat energy absorbed in process of changing form of substance without change in temperature or pressure.
9. Reduction in pressure below atmospheric pressure.
14. A standard unit of measure for electrical resistance.

A. Vacuum	B. Montreal Protocol	C. Line Set	D. OHM
E. Therm	F. Decibel	G. Refrigerant circuit	H. Halide Refrigerants
I. Accumulator	J. Partial Pressure	K. Charles Law	L. Latent Heat
M. High pressure	N. Vapor	O. Reclaim	P. Leak Detector
Q. Evaporator	R. Junction Box	S. Damper	

12. Using the Across and Down clues, write the correct words in the numbered grid below.

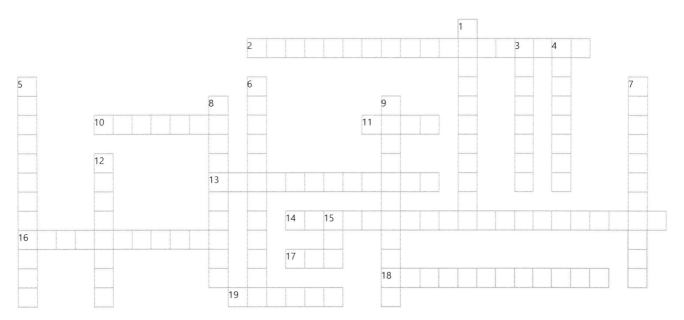

ACROSS

2. Volume displaced by piston as it travels length of stroke.
10. The piping used to connect the outdoor unit to the indoor unit.
11. Unit of electrical power.
13. Typically, a multi ported valve used by service technicians to isolate remote system components, as well as check pressures and charge refrigerating units.
14. Breaks down the CFCs and frees the chlorine ion at stratosphere.
16. A refrigerant has a boiling point above 10C or 50F at atmospheric pressure.
17. A radial or axial flow device used for moving or producing artificial currents of air.
18. In flowing fluid, height of fluid equivalent to its velocity pressure.
19. The SI base unit of temperature; a unit on an absolute temperature scale.

DOWN

1. Instrument used to measure pressures below atmospheric pressure.
3. Forming a homogeneous mixture of liquids when added together.
4. Gas used for leak detection.
5. A passive throttling device, comprised of a small opening, located upstream of the evaporator.
6. Pressure which exists in condensing side of refrigerating system.
7. Type of torch used to detect halogen refrigerant leaks.
8. A unit of Pressure equal to exactly 760 mmHg
9. Self piercing valve body designed to be permanently silver brazed or clamped to refrigerant tubing surface.
12. A solution or surface that is capable of soaking up (taking in) another substance or energy form.
15. A unit of measurement used for determining cooling capacity. One ton is the equivalent of 12,000 BTUs per hour.

A. Line Set	B. Piston Displacement	C. Absorber	D. Atmosphere
E. Saddle Valve	F. TON	G. Fan	H. Service Valve
I. Watt	J. Halide Torch	K. Orifice Plate	L. Velocity Head
M. Head Pressure	N. Low pressure	O. Ultraviolet Radiation	P. Miscible
Q. Kelvin	R. Vacuum Gauge	S. Nitrogen	

13. Using the Across and Down clues, write the correct words in the numbered grid below.

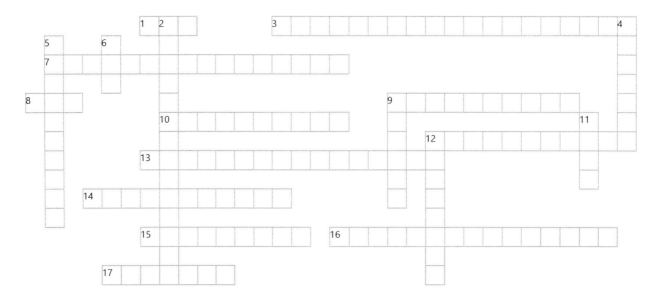

ACROSS

1. A radial or axial flow device used for moving or producing artificial currents of air.
3. Pressure operated control which opens electrical circuit if high side pressure becomes excessive.
7. Gauge pressure plus atmospheric pressure (14.7 lbs. per sq. in.).
8. High Pressure
9. Special high efficiency device (pump) used create deep vacuum within an AC
10. A mechanism that removes flash gas from the evaporator.
12. A substance produces a refrigerating or cooling effect while expanding or vaporizing.
13. A refrigerant has a boiling point below minus 50C or minus 58F at atmospheric pressure.
14. A form of testing for high pressure cylinders.
15. Latin for the least amount of Refrigerant you can release into the atmosphere.
16. Requires the assistance of components such as the appliance or unit's compressor to remove the refrigerant from the appliance.
17. To extract refrigerant from an appliance and clean refrigerant for reuse without meeting all of the requirements for reclamation.

DOWN

2. Equipment that has its own compressor or pump.
4. The piping used to connect the outdoor unit to the indoor unit.
5. Heat energy absorbed in process of changing form of substance without change in temperature or pressure.
6. A unit of measurement used for determining cooling capacity. One ton is the equivalent of 12,000 BTUs per hour.
9. Reduction in pressure below atmospheric pressure.
11. Unit of electrical power.
12. Receives high pressure liquid from the condenser

A. Fan
B. Head Pressure Control
C. Passive recovery
D. Econimizer
E. De Minimus
F. Active recovery
G. Hydrostatic
H. Refrigerant
I. Red
J. Line Set
K. Receiver
L. Very high pressure
M. TON
N. Latent Heat
O. Absolute Pressure
P. Recycle
Q. Vacuum Pump
R. Vacuum
S. Watt

14. Using the Across and Down clues, write the correct words in the numbered grid below.

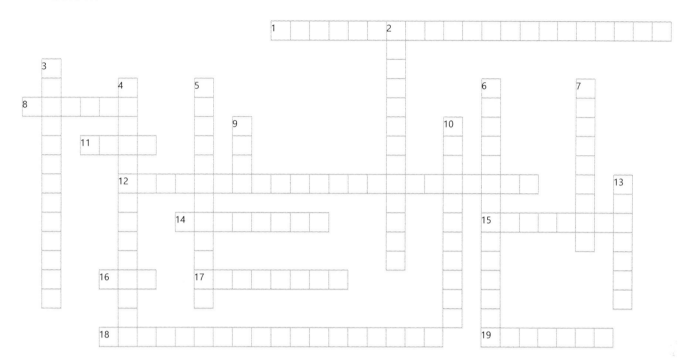

ACROSS

1. Need to evacuate system to eliminate air and moisture at the end of service.
8. Reduction in pressure below atmospheric pressure.
11. Electrical "pressure" applied to a circuit.
12. Refrigerator which creates low temperatures by using the cooling effect formed when a refrigerant is absorbed by chemical substance.
14. High-efficiency design motor used on virtually all of today's HVAC & R equipment requiring motors.
15. That time period of a refrigeration cycle when the system is not operating.
16. A radial or axial flow device used for moving or producing artificial currents of air.
17. Receives high pressure liquid from the condenser
18. The parts of an appliance that are normally connected to each other and are designed to contain refrigerant.
19. To remove refrigerant in any condition from an appliance and store it in an external container without necessarily testing or processing it in any way.

DOWN

2. Condition in which refrigerant and
3. A separation process in which a certain quantity of a mixture is divided during a phase transition
4. Any products that are fully manufactured, charged, and hermetically sealed in a factory with five pounds or less of refrigerant
5. Pressure which exists in condensing side of refrigerating system.
6. An AC motor which operates on principle of rotating magnetic field. Rotor has no electrical connection, but receives electrical energy by transformer action from field windings.
7. Any device which contains a refrigerant and which is used for household or commercial purposes, including any air conditioner, refrigerator, chiller, or freezer.
9. Invisible energy caused by the motion of molecules within any substance or matter.
10. A form of testing for high pressure cylinders.
13. Any maintenance or repair on an appliance that would release refrigerant from the appliance to the atmosphere.

A. Heat
B. Hydrostatic
C. Refrigerant circuit
D. Off Cycle
E. Small appliance
F. Receiver
G. Recover
H. Fan
I. Volt
J. PSC Motor
K. Dehydration Evacuation
L. Absorption Refrigerator
M. Acid Condition
N. Appliance
O. Fractionation
P. Vacuum
Q. Opening
R. Induction Motor
S. Head Pressure

37

15. Using the Across and Down clues, write the correct words in the numbered grid below.

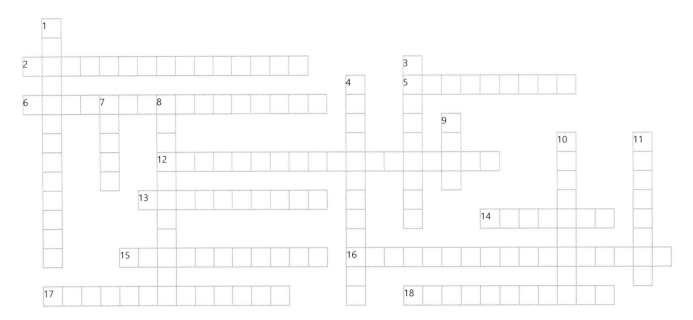

ACROSS

2. Requires the assistance of components such as the appliance or unit's compressor to remove the refrigerant from the appliance.
5. Each refrigerant in the blend keeps its own temperature and pressure characteristics.
6. A refrigerant has a boiling point below minus 50C or minus 58F at atmospheric pressure.
12. The parts of an appliance that are normally connected to each other and are designed to contain refrigerant.
13. A mechanism that removes flash gas from the evaporator.
14. Device used in measurement of relative humidity. Evaporation of moisture lowers temperature of wet bulb compared to dry bulb temperature in same area.
15. The temperature at which the non-azeotropic blend first begins to evaporate.
16. Gray cylinder with a yellow top; used for recovery or transporting refrigerant.
17. Condition in which refrigerant and
18. Property of non-conductor that permits storage of electrical energy in an electrostatic field.

DOWN

1. A device for the transfer of heat energy from the source to the conveying medium, with the latter often being air or water.
3. A mixture of at least two different liquids.
4. Control used to open or close electrical circuits as temperature or pressure limits are reached.
7. A chemical used in fire extinguishing.
8. A compound containing only the elements hydrogen and carbon.
9. Low pressure
10. The process whereby a gas spreads out through another gas to occupy the space with uniform partial Pressure.
11. Round or rectangular pipes or controlled paths acting as conduit for return, mixed, makeup, supply or exhaust air.

A. Diffusion
B. Reusable cylinders
C. Hydrocarbon
D. Zeotropic
E. Econimizer
F. Very high pressure
G. Blue
H. Acid Condition
I. Limit Control
J. Ductwork
K. Azeotroph
L. Passive recovery
M. Capacitance
N. Halon
O. Wet Bulb
P. Heat Exchanger
Q. Refrigerant circuit
R. Bubble Point

16. Using the Across and Down clues, write the correct words in the numbered grid below.

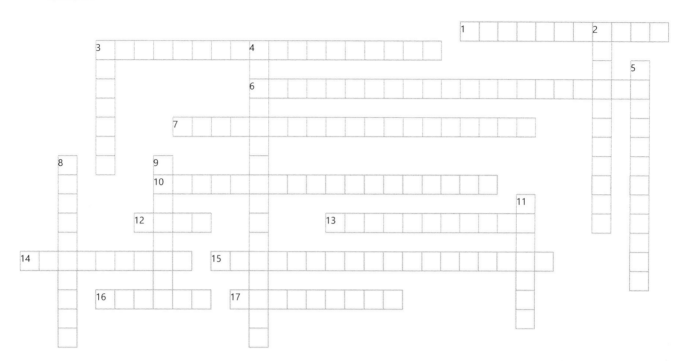

ACROSS

1. Self piercing valve body designed to be permanently silver brazed or clamped to refrigerant tubing surface.
3. The parts of an appliance that are normally connected to each other and are designed to contain refrigerant.
6. The temperature where a refrigerant exists in both liquid and vapor form relative to its measured pressure.
7. A temperature scale in which the lowest temperature that can be attained theoretically is zero
10. Family of refrigerants containing halogen chemicals.
12. Electrical "pressure" applied to a circuit.
13. Degree of hotness or coldness as measured by a thermometer
14. Each refrigerant in the blend keeps its own temperature and pressure characteristics.
15. Represents the amount of energy required to raise one pound of water one degree Fahrenheit.
16. Unit of measure referring to the flow of electrons within a circuit.
17. A combination shut-off and service value typically used on the inlet and outlet of a compressor.

DOWN

2. Accumulates any low pressure liquid from the evaporator so it can vaporize before entering the compressor
3. Reducing contaminants in the used refrigerant
4. Amount of moisture in the air, indicated in grains per cubic foot.
5. Device or instrument such as a halide torch, an electronic sniffer; or soap solution used to detect leaks.
8. Process whereas additional sensible heat (as opposed to latent heat) is removed from condensed refrigerant liquid prior to the metering device.
9. The atom found in CFC and HCFC refrigerants that destroys ozone in the stratosphere.
11. Unit used for measuring relative loudness of sounds.

A. Decibel
D. Refrigerant circuit
G. Accumulator
J. Leak Detector
M. Halide Refrigerants
P. Volt

B. King Valve
E. Absolute Humidity
H. British Thermal Unit
K. Ampere
N. Zeotropic
Q. Saturation Temperature

C. Absolute Temperature
F. Temperature
I. Saddle Valve
L. Chlorine
O. Sub Cooling
R. Recycle

17. Using the Across and Down clues, write the correct words in the numbered grid below.

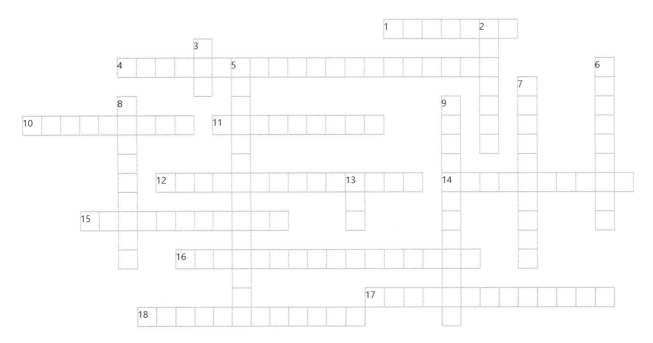

ACROSS

1. Reducing contaminants in the used refrigerant
4. Breaks down the CFCs and frees the chlorine ion at stratosphere.
10. Instrument to measuring pressure of gases and vapors.
11. An independent refrigeration system that separates the non-condensables from the refrigerant and re-condenses and collects any refrigerant in the exhaust vent stream.
12. Chemical compound which is used as a drying agent or desiccant in liquid line filter dryers.
14. A temperature control device. Typically mounted in conditioned space.
15. Property of non-conductor that permits storage of electrical energy in an electrostatic field.
16. Amount of moisture in the air, indicated in grains per cubic foot.
17. Measures low pressure and vacuum.
18. Pressure in low side of refrigerating system; also called suction pressure or low side pressure.

DOWN

2. The piping used to connect the outdoor unit to the indoor unit.
3. The form of matter that is an easily compressible fluid
5. An AC motor which operates on principle of rotating magnetic field. Rotor has no electrical connection, but receives electrical energy by transformer action from field windings.
6. To remove water from a system.
7. A mechanism that removes flash gas from the evaporator.
8. Each refrigerant in the blend keeps its own temperature and pressure characteristics.
9. Control used to open or close electrical circuits as temperature or pressure limits are reached.
13. A radial or axial flow device used for moving or producing artificial currents of air.

A. Manometer
B. Thermostat
C. Limit Control
D. Purge unit
E. Fan
F. Zeotropic
G. Back Pressure
H. Capacitance
I. Calcium Sulfate
J. Compound gauge
K. Absolute Humidity
L. Line Set
M. Gas
N. Induction Motor
O. Recycle
P. Econimizer
Q. Dehydrate
R. Ultraviolet Radiation

18. Using the Across and Down clues, write the correct words in the numbered grid below.

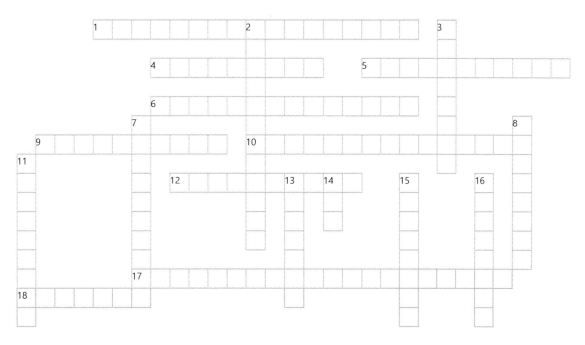

ACROSS

1. A chiller that uses a brine solution and water to provide refrigeration without the aid of a compressor.
4. Light provided with test leads, used to test or probe electrical circuits to determine if they are alive.
5. Device used to measure quantities of heat or determine specific heats.
6. Creates pressure drop to allow liquid refrigerant to boil and absorb latent heat.
9. Any material or substance which has the ability to retard the flow or transfer of heat.
10. Converts high pressure liquid to low pressure vapor
12. To add to speed; hasten progress of development.
17. Breaks down the CFCs and frees the chlorine ion at stratosphere.
18. Any maintenance or repair on an appliance that would release refrigerant from the appliance to the atmosphere.

DOWN

2. A passive throttling device, comprised of a small opening, located upstream of the evaporator.
3. Side by side and having the same distance continuously between them.
7. Device which releases the contents of a container above normal pressures, and before rupture pressures are reached.
8. Receives high pressure liquid from the condenser
11. The process whereby a gas spreads out through another gas to occupy the space with uniform partial Pressure.
13. Reducing contaminants in the used refrigerant
14. A unit of measurement used for determining cooling capacity. One ton is the equivalent of 12,000 BTUs per hour.
15. The temperature at which the non-azeotropic blend first begins to condense.
16. Round or rectangular pipes or controlled paths acting as conduit for return, mixed, makeup, supply or exhaust air.

A. Expansion device	B. TON	C. Accelerate	D. Insulation
E. Absorption Chiller	F. Safety Plug	G. Receiver	H. Calorimeter
I. Diffusion	J. Orifice Plate	K. Ductwork	L. Ultraviolet Radiation
M. Metering Device	N. Dew Point	O. Recycle	P. Parallel
Q. Opening	R. Test Light		

19. Using the Across and Down clues, write the correct words in the numbered grid below.

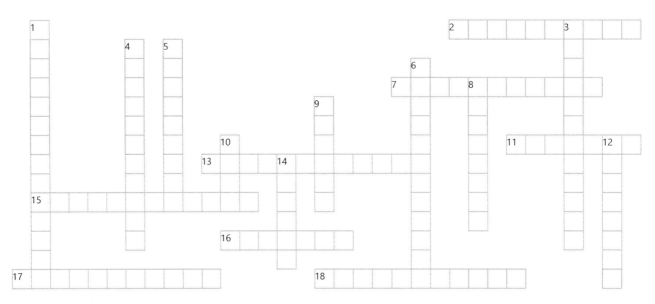

ACROSS

2. Special high efficiency device (pump) used create deep vacuum within an AC
7. Type of torch used to detect halogen refrigerant leaks.
11. To remove refrigerant in any condition from an appliance and store it in an external container without necessarily testing or processing it in any way.
13. Device or instrument such as a halide torch, an electronic sniffer; or soap solution used to detect leaks.
15. Induced currents flowing in a core.
16. The piping used to connect the outdoor unit to the indoor unit.
17. Substance used to counteract acids, in refrigeration system.
18. Fluid opening

DOWN

1. Creates pressure drop to allow liquid refrigerant to boil and absorb latent heat.
3. Either a sling type, or electronic. Instrument used to determine wet bulb temperatures and relative humidity.
4. Instrument used to measure pressures below atmospheric pressure.
5. Instrument to measuring pressure of gases and vapors.
6. Pressure in low side of refrigerating system; also called suction pressure or low side pressure.
8. The temperature at which the non-azeotropic blend first begins to condense.
9. Device for removing small particles from a fluid.
10. Invisible energy caused by the motion of molecules within any substance or matter.
12. The process in which a gas flows through a small hole in a container.
14. Valve for controlling airflow. Found in duct work, movable plate opens and closes to control airflow.

A. Back Pressure	B. Effusion	C. Leak Detector	D. Back Seating
E. Vacuum Gauge	F. Dew Point	G. Eddy Currents	H. Vacuum Pump
I. Metering Device	J. Filter	K. Neutralizer	L. Heat
M. Recover	N. Manometer	O. Psychrometer	P. Line Set
Q. Damper	R. Halide Torch		

20. Using the Across and Down clues, write the correct words in the numbered grid below.

ACROSS

3. The piping used to connect the outdoor unit to the indoor unit.
4. Change in temperature of a gas on expansion through a porous plug from a high pressure to a lower pressure.
7. Requires the assistance of components such as the appliance or unit's compressor to remove the refrigerant from the appliance.
11. A radial or axial flow device used for moving or producing artificial currents of air.
13. A refrigerant has a boiling point below minus 50C or minus 58F at atmospheric pressure.
14. Unit used for measuring relative loudness of sounds.
15. Compressing refrigerant gas without removing or adding heat.
16. The process in which a gas flows through a small hole in a container.
17. Fluid opening

DOWN

1. Part of stator of motor which concentrates magnetic field of field winding.
2. Measures low pressure and vacuum.
5. A form of testing for high pressure cylinders.
6. A device for the transfer of heat energy from the source to the conveying medium, with the latter often being air or water.
8. The moving of heat from an undesirable location, to that of a location where its presence is less undesirable.
9. The Gaseous state of any kind of matter that normally exists as a liquid or solid.
10. Any maintenance or repair on an appliance that would release refrigerant from the appliance to the atmosphere.
12. The temperature at which the non-azeotropic blend first begins to evaporate.

A. Decibel
D. Very high pressure
G. Compound gauge
J. Fan
M. Adiabatic Compression
P. Effusion

B. Line Set
E. Vapor
H. Field Pole
K. Opening
N. Back Seating
Q. Hydrostatic

C. Bubble Point
F. Joule
I. Refrigeration
L. Heat Exchanger
O. Passive recovery

1. Using the Across and Down clues, write the correct words in the numbered grid below.

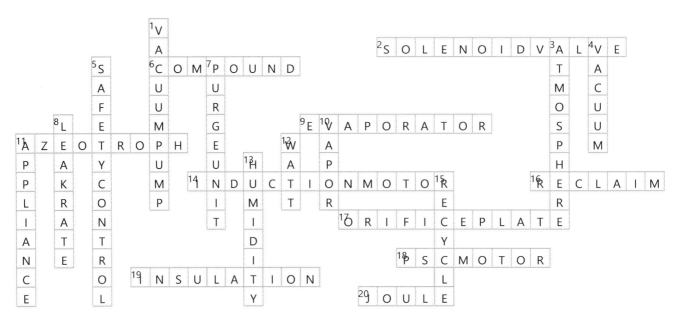

ACROSS

2. Valve actuated by magnetic action by means of an electrically energized coil.
6. A substance formed by a union of two or more elements
9. Evaporates low pressure vapor from the expansion device
11. A mixture of at least two different liquids.
14. An AC motor which operates on principle of rotating magnetic field. Rotor has no electrical connection, but receives electrical energy by transformer action from field windings.
16. Converting recycled refrigerant into a product to be reused.
17. A passive throttling device, comprised of a small opening, located upstream of the evaporator.
18. High-efficiency design motor used on virtually all of today's HVAC & R equipment requiring motors.
19. Any material or substance which has the ability to retard the flow or transfer of heat.
20. Change in temperature of a gas on expansion through a porous plug from a high pressure to a lower pressure.

DOWN

1. Special high efficiency device (pump) used create deep vacuum within an AC
3. A unit of Pressure equal to exactly 760 mmHg
4. Reduction in pressure below atmospheric pressure.
5. Device used to electrically shut down a refrigerating unit when unsafe pressures and
7. An independent refrigeration system that separates the non-condensables from the refrigerant and re-condenses and collects any refrigerant in the exhaust vent stream.
8. The rate at which an appliance is losing refrigerant.
10. Gas phase
11. Any device which contains a refrigerant and which is used for household or commercial purposes, including any air conditioner, refrigerator, chiller, or freezer.
12. Unit of electrical power.
13. The total amount of moisture in air.
15. To extract refrigerant from an appliance and clean refrigerant for reuse without meeting all of the requirements for reclamation.

A. Orifice Plate
B. Recycle
C. Solenoid Valve
D. Vacuum
E. Insulation
F. Induction Motor
G. Joule
H. Watt
I. Leak Rate
J. Azeotroph
K. Vacuum Pump
L. Safety Control
M. Reclaim
N. Evaporator
O. Appliance
P. Purge unit
Q. Compound
R. Atmosphere
S. Humidity
T. Vapor
U. PSC Motor

2. Using the Across and Down clues, write the correct words in the numbered grid below.

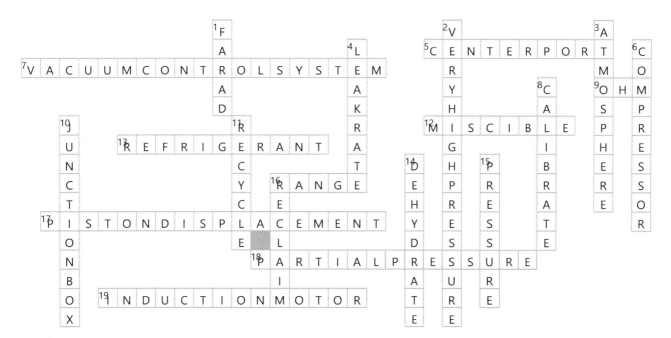

ACROSS

5. Connects manifold to recovery device.
7. In some air conditioning systems, vacuum is used to operate dampers and controls in system.
9. A standard unit of measure for electrical resistance.
12. Forming a homogeneous mixture of liquids when added together.
13. The fluid used for heat transfer in a refrigeration system, which absorbs heat during evaporation at low temperature and pressure, and releases heat during condensation.
16. Pressure or temperature settings of a control; change within limits.
17. Volume displaced by piston as it travels length of stroke.
18. The Pressure exerted by a particular Gas in a mixture.
19. An AC motor which operates on principle of rotating magnetic field. Rotor has no electrical connection, but receives electrical energy by transformer action from field windings.

DOWN

1. Unit of electrical capacity; capacity of a condenser which, when charged with one coulomb of electricity, gives difference of potential of one volt.
2. A refrigerant has a boiling point below minus 50C or minus 58F at atmospheric pressure.
3. A unit of Pressure equal to exactly 760 mmHg
4. The rate at which an appliance is losing refrigerant.
6. The heart or "pump" within an air conditioning or heat pump system.
8. To determine; position indicators as required to obtain accurate measurements.
10. Group of electrical terminals housed in protective box or container.
11. Reducing contaminants in the used refrigerant
14. To remove water from a system.
15. The force exerted per unit area of surface.
16. Converting recycled refrigerant into a product to be reused.

A. Atmosphere	B. Induction Motor	C. OHM
D. Dehydrate	E. Leak Rate	F. Partial Pressure
G. Vacuum Control System	H. Piston Displacement	I. Compressor
J. Refrigerant	K. Very high pressure	L. Center port
M. Pressure	N. Range	O. Junction Box
P. Calibrate	Q. Miscible	R. Reclaim
S. Recycle	T. Farad	

3. Using the Across and Down clues, write the correct words in the numbered grid below.

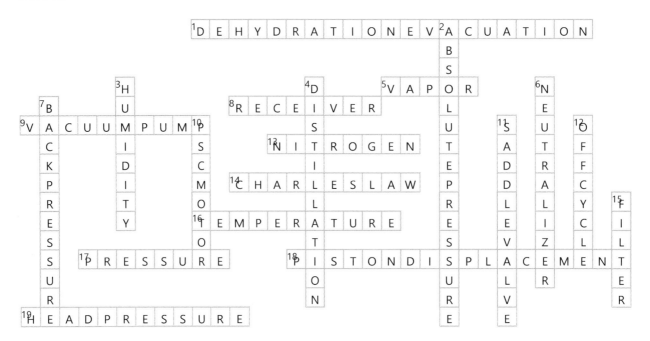

ACROSS

1. Need to evacuate system to eliminate air and moisture at the end of service.
5. Gas phase
8. Receives high pressure liquid from the condenser
9. Special high efficiency device (pump) used create deep vacuum within an AC
13. Gas used for leak detection.
14. States that the volume occupied by a gas at a constant Pressure is directly proportional to the absolute temperature.
16. Degree of hotness or coldness as measured by a thermometer
17. The force exerted per unit area of surface.
18. Volume displaced by piston as it travels length of stroke.
19. Pressure which exists in condensing side of refrigerating system.

DOWN

2. Gauge pressure plus atmospheric pressure (14.7 lbs. per sq. in.).
3. The total amount of moisture in air.
4. The action of purifying a liquid by a process of heating and cooling.
6. Substance used to counteract acids, in refrigeration system.
7. Pressure in low side of refrigerating system; also called suction pressure or low side pressure.
10. High-efficiency design motor used on virtually all of today's HVAC & R equipment requiring motors.
11. Self piercing valve body designed to be permanently silver brazed or clamped to refrigerant tubing surface.
12. That time period of a refrigeration cycle when the system is not operating.
15. Device for removing small particles from a fluid.

A. Filter
B. Vacuum Pump
C. Absolute Pressure
D. Head Pressure
E. Saddle Valve
F. Pressure
G. Vapor
H. Back Pressure
I. Charles Law
J. Neutralizer
K. Distillation
L. Temperature
M. Nitrogen
N. Dehydration Evacuation
O. PSC Motor
P. Off Cycle
Q. Humidity
R. Piston Displacement
S. Receiver

4. Using the Across and Down clues, write the correct words in the numbered grid below.

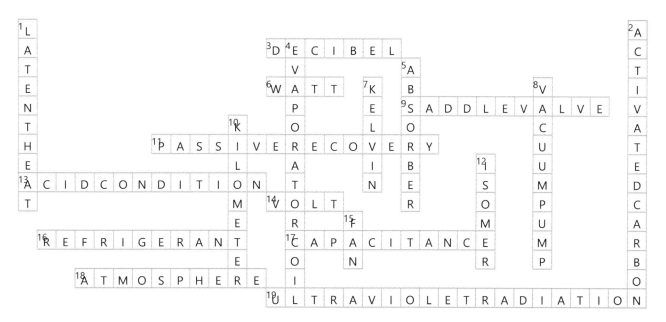

ACROSS

3. Unit used for measuring relative loudness of sounds.
6. Unit of electrical power.
9. Self piercing valve body designed to be permanently silver brazed or clamped to refrigerant tubing surface.
11. Requires the assistance of components such as the appliance or unit's compressor to remove the refrigerant from the appliance.
13. Condition in which refrigerant and
14. Electrical "pressure" applied to a circuit.
16. A substance produces a refrigerating or cooling effect while expanding or vaporizing.
17. Property of non-conductor that permits storage of electrical energy in an electrostatic field.
18. A unit of Pressure equal to exactly 760 mmHg
19. Breaks down the CFCs and frees the chlorine ion at stratosphere.

DOWN

1. Heat energy absorbed in process of changing form of substance without change in temperature or pressure.
2. Specially processed carbon used as a filter drier; commonly used to clean air.
4. Where heat is absorbed by warm air passing across. Liquid refrigerant boils as it is metered into coil, and changes from liquid to vapor.
5. A solution or surface that is capable of soaking up (taking in) another substance or energy form.
7. The SI base unit of temperature; a unit on an absolute temperature scale.
8. Special high efficiency device (pump) used create deep vacuum within an AC
10. Unit of electrical power, equal to 1000 watts.
12. One of a group of substances having the same combination of elements but arranged spatially in different ways.
15. A radial or axial flow device used for moving or producing artificial currents of air.

A. Saddle Valve	B. Fan	C. Watt	D. Passive recovery
E. Kilometer	F. Evaporator Coil	G. Acid Condition	H. Decibel
I. Refrigerant	J. Ultraviolet Radiation	K. Atmosphere	L. Isomer
M. Latent Heat	N. Absorber	O. Capacitance	P. Activated Carbon
Q. Vacuum Pump	R. Volt	S. Kelvin	

5. Using the Across and Down clues, write the correct words in the numbered grid below.

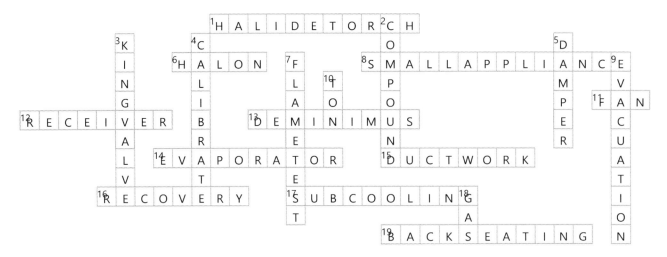

ACROSS

1. Type of torch used to detect halogen refrigerant leaks.
6. A chemical used in fire extinguishing.
8. Any products that are fully manufactured, charged, and hermetically sealed in a factory with five pounds or less of refrigerant
11. A radial or axial flow device used for moving or producing artificial currents of air.
12. Receives high pressure liquid from the condenser
13. Latin for the least amount of Refrigerant you can release into the atmosphere.
14. Evaporates low pressure vapor from the expansion device
15. Round or rectangular pipes or controlled paths acting as conduit for return, mixed, makeup, supply or exhaust air.
16. The process of collecting used refrigerant.
17. Process whereas additional sensible heat (as opposed to latent heat) is removed from condensed refrigerant liquid prior to the metering device.
19. Fluid opening

DOWN

2. A substance formed by a union of two or more elements
3. A combination shut-off and service value typically used on the inlet and outlet of a compressor.
4. To determine; position indicators as required to obtain accurate measurements.
5. Valve for controlling airflow. Found in duct work, movable plate opens and closes to control airflow.
7. Tool which is principally a torch and when an air refrigerant mixture is fed to flame, this flame will change color in presence of heated copper.
9. The process of extracting any air, non-condensable gases, or water from the system.
10. A unit of measurement used for determining cooling capacity. One ton is the equivalent of 12,000 BTUs per hour.
18. Vapor phase or state of a substance.

A. Flame Test	B. De Minimus	C. Sub Cooling	D. Calibrate
E. Ductwork	F. Damper	G. Small appliance	H. Halide Torch
I. Evacuation	J. Evaporator	K. Fan	L. Halon
M. Compound	N. Recovery	O. Receiver	P. King Valve
Q. TON	R. Gas	S. Back Seating	

6. Using the Across and Down clues, write the correct words in the numbered grid below.

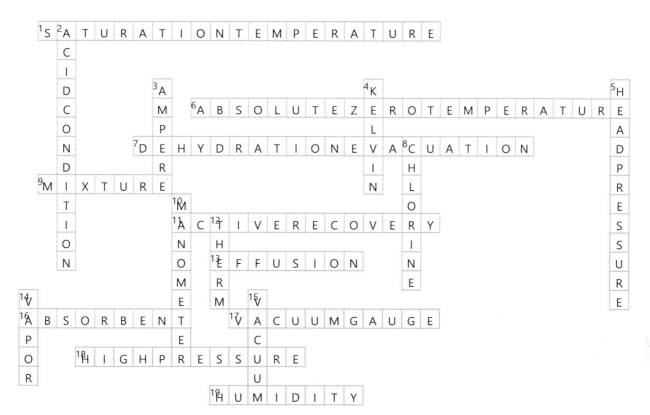

ACROSS

1. The temperature where a refrigerant exists in both liquid and vapor form relative to its measured pressure.
6. Temperature at which molecular motion ceases.
7. Need to evacuate system to eliminate air and moisture at the end of service.
9. A blend of two or more components that do not a have fixed proportion to one another.
11. Equipment that has its own compressor or pump.
13. The process in which a gas flows through a small hole in a container.
16. Substance with ability to take up, or absorb another substance.
17. Instrument used to measure pressures below atmospheric pressure.
18. A refrigerant has a boiling point between minus 50C and 10C degrees at atmospheric pressure.
19. The total amount of moisture in air.

DOWN

2. Condition in which refrigerant and
3. Unit of measure referring to the flow of electrons within a circuit.
4. The SI base unit of temperature; a unit on an absolute temperature scale.
5. Pressure which exists in condensing side of refrigerating system.
8. The atom found in CFC and HCFC refrigerants that destroys ozone in the stratosphere.
10. Instrument to measuring pressure of gases and vapors.
12. Quantity of heat equivalent to 100,000 Btu.
14. The Gaseous state of any kind of matter that normally exists as a liquid or solid.
15. Reduction in pressure below atmospheric pressure.

A. Head Pressure
B. Mixture
C. Ampere
D. Vacuum
E. Absolute Zero Temperature
F. Chlorine
G. Therm
H. Acid Condition
I. Dehydration Evacuation
J. Humidity
K. Vapor
L. Absorbent
M. Manometer
N. Vacuum Gauge
O. Effusion
P. Active recovery
Q. Kelvin
R. High pressure
S. Saturation Temperature

7. Using the Across and Down clues, write the correct words in the numbered grid below.

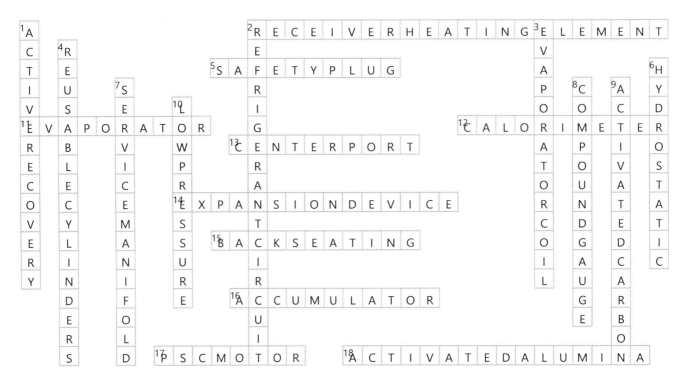

ACROSS

2. Electrical resistance mounted in or around liquid receiver, used to maintain head pressures when ambient temperature is at freezing or below freezing.
5. Device which releases the contents of a container above normal pressures, and before rupture pressures are reached.
11. Evaporates low pressure vapor from the expansion device
12. Device used to measure quantities of heat or determine specific heats.
13. Connects manifold to recovery device.
14. Converts high pressure liquid to low pressure vapor
15. Fluid opening
16. Accumulates any low pressure liquid from the evaporator so it can vaporize before entering the compressor
17. High-efficiency design motor used on virtually all of today's HVAC & R equipment requiring motors.
18. Chemical used as a drier or desiccant.

DOWN

1. Equipment that has its own compressor or pump.
2. The parts of an appliance that are normally connected to each other and are designed to contain refrigerant.
3. Where heat is absorbed by warm air passing across. Liquid refrigerant boils as it is metered into coil, and changes from liquid to vapor.
4. Gray cylinder with a yellow top; used for recovery or transporting refrigerant.
6. A form of testing for high pressure cylinders.
7. A device equipped with gauges and manual valves, used by serviceman to service refrigerating systems.
8. Measures low pressure and vacuum.
9. Specially processed carbon used as a filter drier; commonly used to clean air.
10. A refrigerant has a boiling point above 10C or 50F at atmospheric pressure.

A. Compound gauge
D. Calorimeter
G. Receiver Heating Element
J. Evaporator
M. Reusable cylinders
P. Accumulator
S. PSC Motor

B. Refrigerant circuit
E. Center port
H. Active recovery
K. Activated Carbon
N. Activated Alumina
Q. Service Manifold

C. Evaporator Coil
F. Hydrostatic
I. Back Seating
L. Safety Plug
O. Low pressure
R. Expansion device

50

8. Using the Across and Down clues, write the correct words in the numbered grid below.

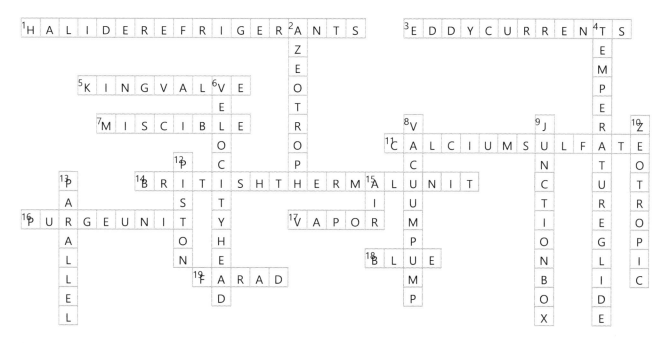

ACROSS

1. Family of refrigerants containing halogen chemicals.
3. Induced currents flowing in a core.
5. A combination shut-off and service value typically used on the inlet and outlet of a compressor.
7. Forming a homogeneous mixture of liquids when added together.
11. Chemical compound which is used as a drying agent or desiccant in liquid line filter dryers.
14. Represents the amount of energy required to raise one pound of water one degree Fahrenheit.
16. An independent refrigeration system that separates the non-condensables from the refrigerant and re-condenses and collects any refrigerant in the exhaust vent stream.
17. Gas phase
18. Low pressure
19. Unit of electrical capacity; capacity of a condenser which, when charged with one coulomb of electricity, gives difference of potential of one volt.

DOWN

2. A mixture of at least two different liquids.
4. The difference between the Dew Point and the Bubble Point.
6. In flowing fluid, height of fluid equivalent to its velocity pressure.
8. Special high efficiency device (pump) used create deep vacuum within an AC
9. Group of electrical terminals housed in protective box or container.
10. Each refrigerant in the blend keeps its own temperature and pressure characteristics.
12. Close fitting part which moves up and down in a cylinder.
13. Side by side and having the same distance continuously between them.
15. Invisible, odorless, and tasteless mixture of gases which form earth's atmosphere.

A. Purge unit	B. Miscible	C. Farad	D. Junction Box
E. Blue	F. Temperature Glide	G. Vapor	H. Velocity Head
I. Zeotropic	J. Halide Refrigerants	K. Eddy Currents	L. Air
M. Vacuum Pump	N. Azeotroph	O. King Valve	P. British Thermal Unit
Q. Calcium Sulfate	R. Parallel	S. Piston	

9. Using the Across and Down clues, write the correct words in the numbered grid below.

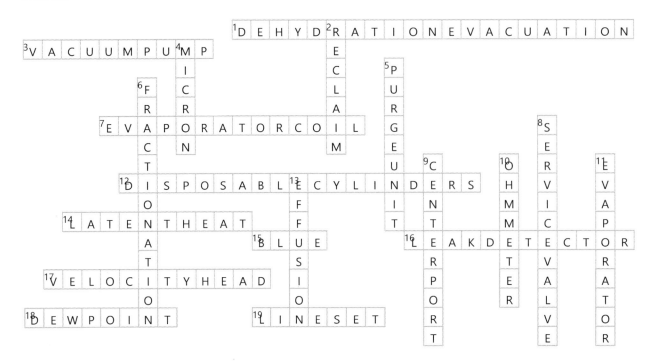

ACROSS

1. Need to evacuate system to eliminate air and moisture at the end of service.
3. Special high efficiency device (pump) used create deep vacuum within an AC
7. Where heat is absorbed by warm air passing across. Liquid refrigerant boils as it is metered into coil, and changes from liquid to vapor.
12. Single use cylinders. Empty cylinders should have the pressure reduced to zero and the cylinder rendered unusable.
14. Heat energy absorbed in process of changing form of substance without change in temperature or pressure.
15. Low pressure
16. Device or instrument such as a halide torch, an electronic sniffer; or soap solution used to detect leaks.
17. In flowing fluid, height of fluid equivalent to its velocity pressure.
18. The temperature at which the non-azeotropic blend first begins to condense.
19. The piping used to connect the outdoor unit to the indoor unit.

DOWN

2. Converting recycled refrigerant into a product to be reused.
4. One thousandth of a millimeter.
5. An independent refrigeration system that separates the non-condensables from the refrigerant and re-condenses and collects any refrigerant in the exhaust vent stream.
6. A separation process in which a certain quantity of a mixture is divided during a phase transition
8. Typically, a multi ported valve used by service technicians to isolate remote system components, as well as check pressures and charge refrigerating units.
9. Connects manifold to recovery device.
10. An instrument for measuring resistance in ohms.
11. Evaporates low pressure vapor from the expansion device
13. The process in which a gas flows through a small hole in a container.

A. Center port
B. Dew Point
C. Vacuum Pump
D. Evaporator
E. Purge unit
F. Disposable cylinders
G. Reclaim
H. Line Set
I. Evaporator Coil
J. Leak Detector
K. Effusion
L. Blue
M. Fractionation
N. Latent Heat
O. Micron
P. Ohmmeter
Q. Service Valve
R. Dehydration Evacuation
S. Velocity Head

10. Using the Across and Down clues, write the correct words in the numbered grid below.

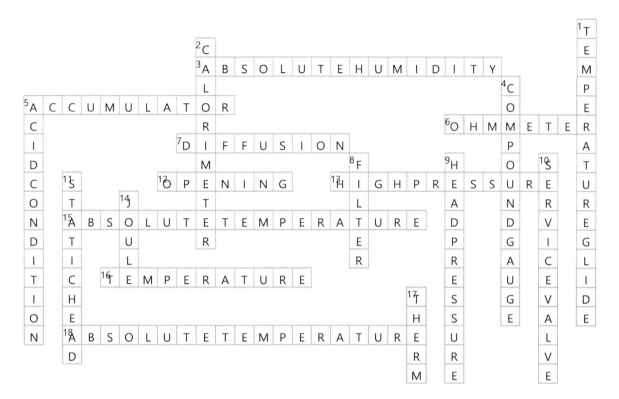

ACROSS

3. Amount of moisture in the air, indicated in grains per cubic foot.
5. Storage tank which receives liquid refrigerant from evaporator and prevents it from flowing into suction line.
6. An instrument for measuring resistance in ohms.
7. The process whereby a gas spreads out through another gas to occupy the space with uniform partial Pressure.
12. Any maintenance or repair on an appliance that would release refrigerant from the appliance to the atmosphere.
13. A refrigerant has a boiling point between minus 50C and 10C degrees at atmospheric pressure.
15. A temperature scale in which the lowest temperature that can be attained theoretically is zero
16. Degree of hotness or coldness as measured by a thermometer
18. Temperature measured from absolute zero.

DOWN

1. The difference between the Dew Point and the Bubble Point.
2. Device used to measure quantities of heat or determine specific heats.
4. Measures low pressure and vacuum.
5. Condition in which refrigerant and
8. Device for removing small particles from a fluid.
9. Pressure which exists in condensing side of refrigerating system.
10. Typically, a multi ported valve used by service technicians to isolate remote system components, as well as check pressures and charge refrigerating units.
11. Pressure of fluid expressed in terms of height of column of the fluid, such as water or mercury.
14. Change in temperature of a gas on expansion through a porous plug from a high pressure to a lower pressure.
17. Quantity of heat equivalent to 100,000 Btu.

A. Absolute Temperature
B. Temperature Glide
C. Absolute Humidity
D. Absolute Temperature
E. Filter
F. Therm
G. Acid Condition
H. Service Valve
I. Temperature
J. Diffusion
K. Accumulator
L. Joule
M. Head Pressure
N. Compound gauge
O. Opening
P. Calorimeter
Q. Static Head
R. Ohmmeter
S. High pressure

11. Using the Across and Down clues, write the correct words in the numbered grid below.

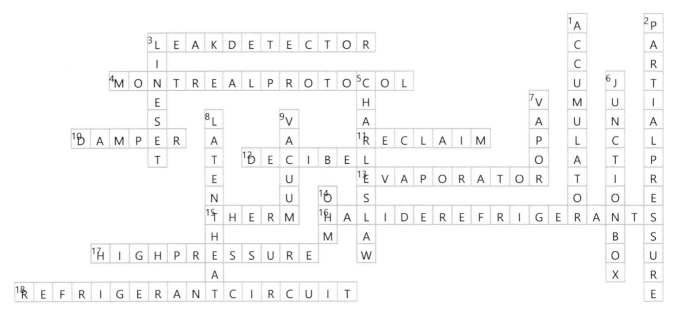

ACROSS

3. Device or instrument such as a halide torch, an electronic sniffer; or soap solution used to detect leaks.
4. Treaty among nations designed to protect the stratospheric ozone layer.
10. Valve for controlling airflow. Found in duct work, movable plate opens and closes to control airflow.
11. Converting recycled refrigerant into a product to be reused.
12. Unit used for measuring relative loudness of sounds.
13. Evaporates low pressure vapor from the expansion device
15. Quantity of heat equivalent to 100,000 Btu.
16. Family of refrigerants containing halogen chemicals.
17. A refrigerant has a boiling point between minus 50C and 10C degrees at atmospheric pressure.
18. The parts of an appliance that are normally connected to each other and are designed to contain refrigerant.

DOWN

1. Storage tank which receives liquid refrigerant from evaporator and prevents it from flowing into suction line.
2. The Pressure exerted by a particular Gas in a mixture.
3. The piping used to connect the outdoor unit to the indoor unit.
5. States that the volume occupied by a gas at a constant Pressure is directly proportional to the absolute temperature.
6. Group of electrical terminals housed in protective box or container.
7. The Gaseous state of any kind of matter that normally exists as a liquid or solid.
8. Heat energy absorbed in process of changing form of substance without change in temperature or pressure.
9. Reduction in pressure below atmospheric pressure.
14. A standard unit of measure for electrical resistance.

A. Vacuum
E. Therm
I. Accumulator
M. High pressure
Q. Evaporator
B. Montreal Protocol
F. Decibel
J. Partial Pressure
N. Vapor
R. Junction Box
C. Line Set
G. Refrigerant circuit
K. Charles Law
O. Reclaim
S. Damper
D. OHM
H. Halide Refrigerants
L. Latent Heat
P. Leak Detector

12. Using the Across and Down clues, write the correct words in the numbered grid below.

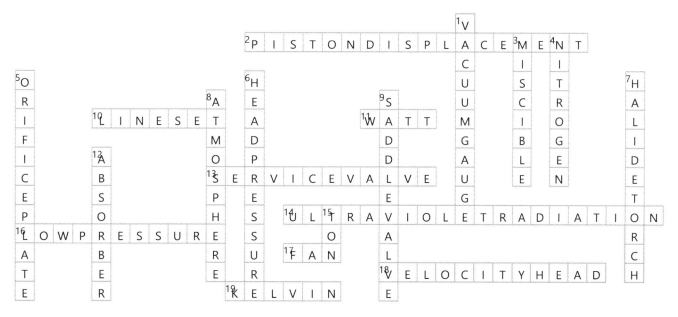

ACROSS

2. Volume displaced by piston as it travels length of stroke.
10. The piping used to connect the outdoor unit to the indoor unit.
11. Unit of electrical power.
13. Typically, a multi ported valve used by service technicians to isolate remote system components, as well as check pressures and charge refrigerating units.
14. Breaks down the CFCs and frees the chlorine ion at stratosphere.
16. A refrigerant has a boiling point above 10C or 50F at atmospheric pressure.
17. A radial or axial flow device used for moving or producing artificial currents of air.
18. In flowing fluid, height of fluid equivalent to its velocity pressure.
19. The SI base unit of temperature; a unit on an absolute temperature scale.

DOWN

1. Instrument used to measure pressures below atmospheric pressure.
3. Forming a homogeneous mixture of liquids when added together.
4. Gas used for leak detection.
5. A passive throttling device, comprised of a small opening, located upstream of the evaporator.
6. Pressure which exists in condensing side of refrigerating system.
7. Type of torch used to detect halogen refrigerant leaks.
8. A unit of Pressure equal to exactly 760 mmHg.
9. Self piercing valve body designed to be permanently silver brazed or clamped to refrigerant tubing surface.
12. A solution or surface that is capable of soaking up (taking in) another substance or energy form.
15. A unit of measurement used for determining cooling capacity. One ton is the equivalent of 12,000 BTUs per hour.

A. Line Set
B. Piston Displacement
C. Absorber
D. Atmosphere
E. Saddle Valve
F. TON
G. Fan
H. Service Valve
I. Watt
J. Halide Torch
K. Orifice Plate
L. Velocity Head
M. Head Pressure
N. Low pressure
O. Ultraviolet Radiation
P. Miscible
Q. Kelvin
R. Vacuum Gauge
S. Nitrogen

13. Using the Across and Down clues, write the correct words in the numbered grid below.

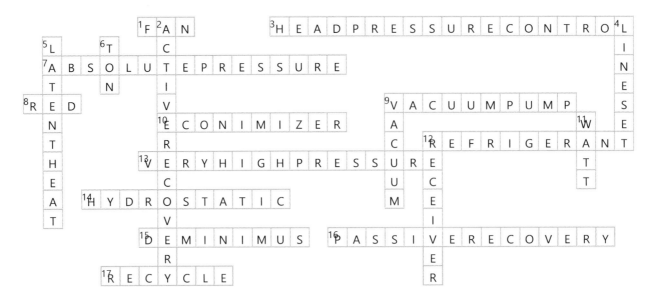

ACROSS

1. A radial or axial flow device used for moving or producing artificial currents of air.
3. Pressure operated control which opens electrical circuit if high side pressure becomes excessive.
7. Gauge pressure plus atmospheric pressure (14.7 lbs. per sq. in.).
8. High Pressure
9. Special high efficiency device (pump) used create deep vacuum within an AC
10. A mechanism that removes flash gas from the evaporator.
12. A substance produces a refrigerating or cooling effect while expanding or vaporizing.
13. A refrigerant has a boiling point below minus 50C or minus 58F at atmospheric pressure.
14. A form of testing for high pressure cylinders.
15. Latin for the least amount of Refrigerant you can release into the atmosphere.
16. Requires the assistance of components such as the appliance or unit's compressor to remove the refrigerant from the appliance.
17. To extract refrigerant from an appliance and clean refrigerant for reuse without meeting all of the requirements for reclamation.

DOWN

2. Equipment that has its own compressor or pump.
4. The piping used to connect the outdoor unit to the indoor unit.
5. Heat energy absorbed in process of changing form of substance without change in temperature or pressure.
6. A unit of measurement used for determining cooling capacity. One ton is the equivalent of 12,000 BTUs per hour.
9. Reduction in pressure below atmospheric pressure.
11. Unit of electrical power.
12. Receives high pressure liquid from the condenser

A. Fan
D. Econimizer
G. Hydrostatic
J. Line Set
M. TON
P. Recycle
S. Watt

B. Head Pressure Control
E. De Minimus
H. Refrigerant
K. Receiver
N. Latent Heat
Q. Vacuum Pump

C. Passive recovery
F. Active recovery
I. Red
L. Very high pressure
O. Absolute Pressure
R. Vacuum

56

14. Using the Across and Down clues, write the correct words in the numbered grid below.

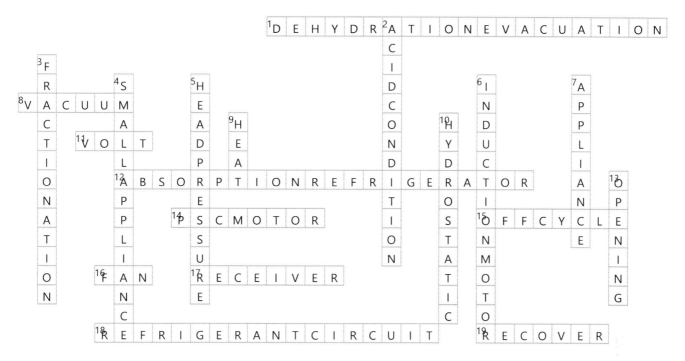

ACROSS

1. Need to evacuate system to eliminate air and moisture at the end of service.
8. Reduction in pressure below atmospheric pressure.
11. Electrical "pressure" applied to a circuit.
12. Refrigerator which creates low temperatures by using the cooling effect formed when a refrigerant is absorbed by chemical substance.
14. High-efficiency design motor used on virtually all of today's HVAC & R equipment requiring motors.
15. That time period of a refrigeration cycle when the system is not operating.
16. A radial or axial flow device used for moving or producing artificial currents of air.
17. Receives high pressure liquid from the condenser
18. The parts of an appliance that are normally connected to each other and are designed to contain refrigerant.
19. To remove refrigerant in any condition from an appliance and store it in an external container without necessarily testing or processing it in any way.

DOWN

2. Condition in which refrigerant and
3. A separation process in which a certain quantity of a mixture is divided during a phase transition
4. Any products that are fully manufactured, charged, and hermetically sealed in a factory with five pounds or less of refrigerant
5. Pressure which exists in condensing side of refrigerating system.
6. An AC motor which operates on principle of rotating magnetic field. Rotor has no electrical connection, but receives electrical energy by transformer action from field windings.
7. Any device which contains a refrigerant and which is used for household or commercial purposes, including any air conditioner, refrigerator, chiller, or freezer.
9. Invisible energy caused by the motion of molecules within any substance or matter.
10. A form of testing for high pressure cylinders.
13. Any maintenance or repair on an appliance that would release refrigerant from the appliance to the atmosphere.

A. Heat
B. Hydrostatic
C. Refrigerant circuit
D. Off Cycle
E. Small appliance
F. Receiver
G. Recover
H. Fan
I. Volt
J. PSC Motor
K. Dehydration Evacuation
L. Absorption Refrigerator
M. Acid Condition
N. Appliance
O. Fractionation
P. Vacuum
Q. Opening
R. Induction Motor
S. Head Pressure

15. Using the Across and Down clues, write the correct words in the numbered grid below.

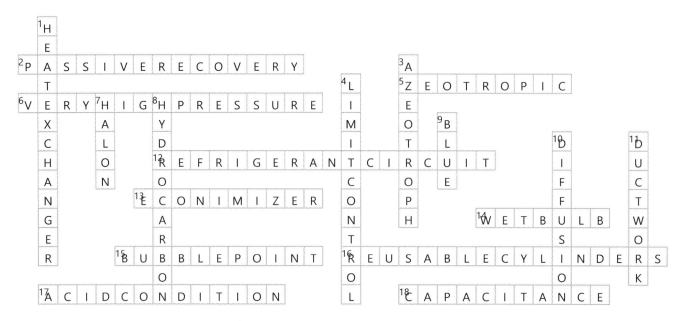

ACROSS

2. Requires the assistance of components such as the appliance or unit's compressor to remove the refrigerant from the appliance.
5. Each refrigerant in the blend keeps its own temperature and pressure characteristics.
6. A refrigerant has a boiling point below minus 50C or minus 58F at atmospheric pressure.
12. The parts of an appliance that are normally connected to each other and are designed to contain refrigerant.
13. A mechanism that removes flash gas from the evaporator.
14. Device used in measurement of relative humidity. Evaporation of moisture lowers temperature of wet bulb compared to dry bulb temperature in same area.
15. The temperature at which the non-azeotropic blend first begins to evaporate.
16. Gray cylinder with a yellow top; used for recovery or transporting refrigerant.
17. Condition in which refrigerant and
18. Property of non-conductor that permits storage of electrical energy in an electrostatic field.

DOWN

1. A device for the transfer of heat energy from the source to the conveying medium, with the latter often being air or water.
3. A mixture of at least two different liquids.
4. Control used to open or close electrical circuits as temperature or pressure limits are reached.
7. A chemical used in fire extinguishing.
8. A compound containing only the elements hydrogen and carbon.
9. Low pressure
10. The process whereby a gas spreads out through another gas to occupy the space with uniform partial Pressure.
11. Round or rectangular pipes or controlled paths acting as conduit for return, mixed, makeup, supply or exhaust air.

A. Diffusion
E. Econimizer
I. Limit Control
M. Capacitance
Q. Refrigerant circuit

B. Reusable cylinders
F. Very high pressure
J. Ductwork
N. Halon
R. Bubble Point

C. Hydrocarbon
G. Blue
K. Azeotroph
O. Wet Bulb

D. Zeotropic
H. Acid Condition
L. Passive recovery
P. Heat Exchanger

16. Using the Across and Down clues, write the correct words in the numbered grid below.

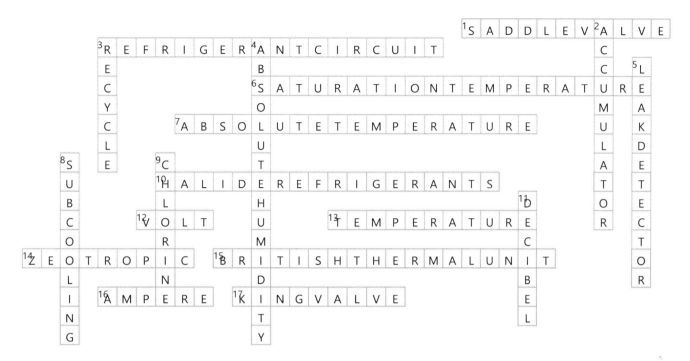

ACROSS

1. Self piercing valve body designed to be permanently silver brazed or clamped to refrigerant tubing surface.
3. The parts of an appliance that are normally connected to each other and are designed to contain refrigerant.
6. The temperature where a refrigerant exists in both liquid and vapor form relative to its measured pressure.
7. A temperature scale in which the lowest temperature that can be attained theoretically is zero
10. Family of refrigerants containing halogen chemicals.
12. Electrical "pressure" applied to a circuit.
13. Degree of hotness or coldness as measured by a thermometer
14. Each refrigerant in the blend keeps its own temperature and pressure characteristics.
15. Represents the amount of energy required to raise one pound of water one degree Fahrenheit.
16. Unit of measure referring to the flow of electrons within a circuit.
17. A combination shut-off and service value typically used on the inlet and outlet of a compressor.

DOWN

2. Accumulates any low pressure liquid from the evaporator so it can vaporize before entering the compressor
3. Reducing contaminants in the used refrigerant
4. Amount of moisture in the air, indicated in grains per cubic foot.
5. Device or instrument such as a halide torch, an electronic sniffer; or soap solution used to detect leaks.
8. Process whereas additional sensible heat (as opposed to latent heat) is removed from condensed refrigerant liquid prior to the metering device.
9. The atom found in CFC and HCFC refrigerants that destroys ozone in the stratosphere.
11. Unit used for measuring relative loudness of sounds.

A. Decibel
D. Refrigerant circuit
G. Accumulator
J. Leak Detector
M. Halide Refrigerants
P. Volt
B. King Valve
E. Absolute Humidity
H. British Thermal Unit
K. Ampere
N. Zeotropic
Q. Saturation Temperature
C. Absolute Temperature
F. Temperature
I. Saddle Valve
L. Chlorine
O. Sub Cooling
R. Recycle

17. Using the Across and Down clues, write the correct words in the numbered grid below.

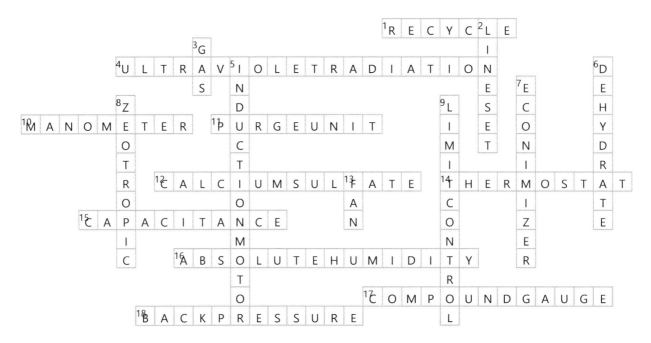

ACROSS

1. Reducing contaminants in the used refrigerant
4. Breaks down the CFCs and frees the chlorine ion at stratosphere.
10. Instrument to measuring pressure of gases and vapors.
11. An independent refrigeration system that separates the non-condensables from the refrigerant and re-condenses and collects any refrigerant in the exhaust vent stream.
12. Chemical compound which is used as a drying agent or desiccant in liquid line filter dryers.
14. A temperature control device. Typically mounted in conditioned space.
15. Property of non-conductor that permits storage of electrical energy in an electrostatic field.
16. Amount of moisture in the air, indicated in grains per cubic foot.
17. Measures low pressure and vacuum.
18. Pressure in low side of refrigerating system; also called suction pressure or low side pressure.

DOWN

2. The piping used to connect the outdoor unit to the indoor unit.
3. The form of matter that is an easily compressible fluid
5. An AC motor which operates on principle of rotating magnetic field. Rotor has no electrical connection, but receives electrical energy by transformer action from field windings.
6. To remove water from a system.
7. A mechanism that removes flash gas from the evaporator.
8. Each refrigerant in the blend keeps its own temperature and pressure characteristics.
9. Control used to open or close electrical circuits as temperature or pressure limits are reached.
13. A radial or axial flow device used for moving or producing artificial currents of air.

A. Manometer
B. Thermostat
C. Limit Control
D. Purge unit
E. Fan
F. Zeotropic
G. Back Pressure
H. Capacitance
I. Calcium Sulfate
J. Compound gauge
K. Absolute Humidity
L. Line Set
M. Gas
N. Induction Motor
O. Recycle
P. Econimizer
Q. Dehydrate
R. Ultraviolet Radiation

18. Using the Across and Down clues, write the correct words in the numbered grid below.

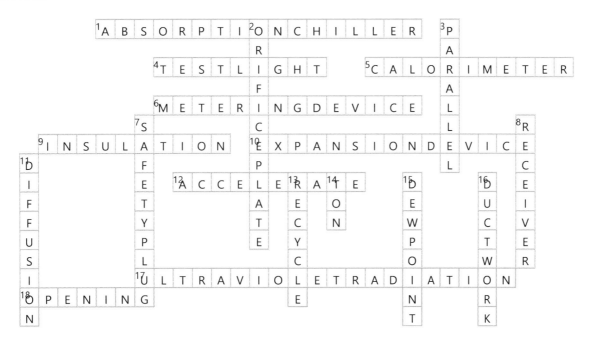

ACROSS

1. A chiller that uses a brine solution and water to provide refrigeration without the aid of a compressor.
4. Light provided with test leads, used to test or probe electrical circuits to determine if they are alive.
5. Device used to measure quantities of heat or determine specific heats.
6. Creates pressure drop to allow liquid refrigerant to boil and absorb latent heat.
9. Any material or substance which has the ability to retard the flow or transfer of heat.
10. Converts high pressure liquid to low pressure vapor
12. To add to speed; hasten progress of development.
17. Breaks down the CFCs and frees the chlorine ion at stratosphere.
18. Any maintenance or repair on an appliance that would release refrigerant from the appliance to the atmosphere.

DOWN

2. A passive throttling device, comprised of a small opening, located upstream of the evaporator.
3. Side by side and having the same distance continuously between them.
7. Device which releases the contents of a container above normal pressures, and before rupture pressures are reached.
8. Receives high pressure liquid from the condenser
11. The process whereby a gas spreads out through another gas to occupy the space with uniform partial Pressure.
13. Reducing contaminants in the used refrigerant
14. A unit of measurement used for determining cooling capacity. One ton is the equivalent of 12,000 BTUs per hour.
15. The temperature at which the non-azeotropic blend first begins to condense.
16. Round or rectangular pipes or controlled paths acting as conduit for return, mixed, makeup, supply or exhaust air.

A. Expansion device
E. Absorption Chiller
I. Diffusion
M. Metering Device
Q. Opening

B. TON
F. Safety Plug
J. Orifice Plate
N. Dew Point
R. Test Light

C. Accelerate
G. Receiver
K. Ductwork
O. Recycle

D. Insulation
H. Calorimeter
L. Ultraviolet Radiation
P. Parallel

19. Using the Across and Down clues, write the correct words in the numbered grid below.

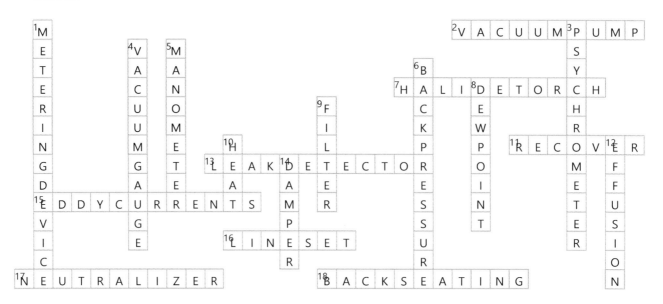

ACROSS

2. Special high efficiency device (pump) used create deep vacuum within an AC
7. Type of torch used to detect halogen refrigerant leaks.
11. To remove refrigerant in any condition from an appliance and store it in an external container without necessarily testing or processing it in any way.
13. Device or instrument such as a halide torch, an electronic sniffer; or soap solution used to detect leaks.
15. Induced currents flowing in a core.
16. The piping used to connect the outdoor unit to the indoor unit.
17. Substance used to counteract acids, in refrigeration system.
18. Fluid opening

DOWN

1. Creates pressure drop to allow liquid refrigerant to boil and absorb latent heat.
3. Either a sling type, or electronic. Instrument used to determine wet bulb temperatures and relative humidity.
4. Instrument used to measure pressures below atmospheric pressure.
5. Instrument to measuring pressure of gases and vapors.
6. Pressure in low side of refrigerating system; also called suction pressure or low side pressure.
8. The temperature at which the non-azeotropic blend first begins to condense.
9. Device for removing small particles from a fluid.
10. Invisible energy caused by the motion of molecules within any substance or matter.
12. The process in which a gas flows through a small hole in a container.
14. Valve for controlling airflow. Found in duct work, movable plate opens and closes to control airflow.

A. Back Pressure
B. Effusion
C. Leak Detector
D. Back Seating
E. Vacuum Gauge
F. Dew Point
G. Eddy Currents
H. Vacuum Pump
I. Metering Device
J. Filter
K. Neutralizer
L. Heat
M. Recover
N. Manometer
O. Psychrometer
P. Line Set
Q. Damper
R. Halide Torch

20. Using the Across and Down clues, write the correct words in the numbered grid below.

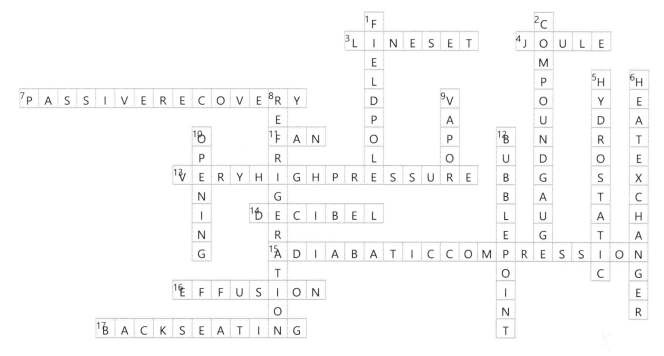

ACROSS

3. The piping used to connect the outdoor unit to the indoor unit.
4. Change in temperature of a gas on expansion through a porous plug from a high pressure to a lower pressure.
7. Requires the assistance of components such as the appliance or unit's compressor to remove the refrigerant from the appliance.
11. A radial or axial flow device used for moving or producing artificial currents of air.
13. A refrigerant has a boiling point below minus 50C or minus 58F at atmospheric pressure.
14. Unit used for measuring relative loudness of sounds.
15. Compressing refrigerant gas without removing or adding heat.
16. The process in which a gas flows through a small hole in a container.
17. Fluid opening

DOWN

1. Part of stator of motor which concentrates magnetic field of field winding.
2. Measures low pressure and vacuum.
5. A form of testing for high pressure cylinders.
6. A device for the transfer of heat energy from the source to the conveying medium, with the latter often being air or water.
8. The moving of heat from an undesirable location, to that of a location where its presence is less undesirable.
9. The Gaseous state of any kind of matter that normally exists as a liquid or solid.
10. Any maintenance or repair on an appliance that would release refrigerant from the appliance to the atmosphere.
12. The temperature at which the non-azeotropic blend first begins to evaporate.

A. Decibel
D. Very high pressure
G. Compound gauge
J. Fan
M. Adiabatic Compression
P. Effusion

B. Line Set
E. Vapor
H. Field Pole
K. Opening
N. Back Seating
Q. Hydrostatic

C. Bubble Point
F. Joule
I. Refrigeration
L. Heat Exchanger
O. Passive recovery

Multiple Choice

A. From the words provided for each clue, provide the letter of the word which best matches the clue.

1. _____ A refrigerant has a boiling point below minus 50C or minus 58F at atmospheric pressure.
   A. Very high pressure   B. Passive recovery   C. Micron   D. Volt

2. _____ The temperature where a refrigerant exists in both liquid and vapor form relative to its measured pressure.
   A. Compound gauge   B. Diffusion   C. Saturation Temperature   D. Vacuum Pump

3. _____ Part of stator of motor which concentrates magnetic field of field winding.
   A. Isomer   B. Acid Condition   C. Absolute Pressure   D. Field Pole

4. _____ Quantity of heat equivalent to 100,000 Btu.
   A. Kelvin   B. Therm   C. Safety Control   D. OHM

5. _____ Temperature at which molecular motion ceases.
   A. Evaporator Coil   B. Vacuum Gauge   C. Absolute Zero Temperature   D. Calcium Sulfate

6. _____ The piping used to connect the outdoor unit to the indoor unit.
   A. Purge unit   B. Evacuation   C. Absolute Humidity   D. Line Set

7. _____ A substance formed by a union of two or more elements
   A. Heat Exchanger   B. Heat   C. Compound   D. Expansion device

8. _____ Condenses high pressure gas from the compressor to high pressure liquid.
   A. Diffusion   B. Activated Carbon   C. Distillation   D. Condenser

9. _____ Gauge pressure plus atmospheric pressure (14.7 lbs. per sq. in.).
   A. Service Manifold   B. Solenoid Valve   C. Absolute Pressure   D. Farad

10. _____ High-efficiency design motor used on virtually all of today's HVAC & R equipment requiring motors.
    A. Gas   B. Off Cycle   C. Pinch off Tool   D. PSC Motor

11. _____ Measures low pressure and vacuum.
    A. Calorimeter   B. Miscible   C. Compound gauge   D. Absolute Temperature

12. _____ Represents the amount of energy required to raise one pound of water one degree Fahrenheit.
    A. Recovery   B. British Thermal Unit   C. Halide Refrigerants   D. Fan

13. _____ Pressure or temperature settings of a control; change within limits.
    A. ACR Tubing   B. Range   C. Pascals Law   D. Service Valve

14. _____ Device used to press walls of a tubing together until fluid flow ceases.
    A. Gauge manifold   B. King Valve   C. Appliance   D. Pinch off Tool

15. _____ The action of purifying a liquid by a process of heating and cooling.
    A. Isolate   B. Distillation   C. Appliance   D. Heat Exchanger

16. _____ Condition in which refrigerant and
    A. Refrigeration   B. Therm   C. Acid Condition   D. Parallel

17. _____ Accumulates any low pressure liquid from the evaporator so it can vaporize before entering the compressor
    A. Temperature   B. Calibrate   C. Adsorbent   D. Accumulator

18. _____ Where heat is absorbed by warm air passing across. Liquid refrigerant boils as it is metered into coil, and changes from liquid to vapor.
    A. Partial Pressure   B. Isolate   C. Insulation   D. Evaporator Coil

19. _____ A device equipped with gauges and manual valves, used by serviceman to service refrigerating systems.
A. Absorbent   B. Service Manifold   C. Adsorption   D. De Minimus

20. _____ Dissipates heat from the refrigerant.
A. Temperature Glide   B. Diffusion   C. Condenser Coil   D. Receiver

21. _____ Creates pressure drop to allow liquid refrigerant to boil and absorb latent heat.
A. Metering Device   B. Latent Heat   C. Ampere   D. Sub Cooling

22. _____ Device used in measurement of relative humidity. Evaporation of moisture lowers temperature of wet bulb compared to dry bulb temperature in same area.
A. Boyles Law   B. Wet Bulb   C. Joule   D. Receiver Heating Element

23. _____ In flowing fluid, height of fluid equivalent to its velocity pressure.
A. Saddle Valve   B. Velocity Head   C. Center port   D. Ohmmeter

24. _____ Tool which is principally a torch and when an air refrigerant mixture is fed to flame, this flame will change color in presence of heated copper.
A. Dehydrate   B. Volt   C. High pressure   D. Flame Test

25. _____ Special high efficiency device (pump) used create deep vacuum within an AC
A. Vapor   B. Zeotropic   C. Vacuum Pump   D. Kilometer

26. _____ Typically, a multi ported valve used by service technicians to isolate remote system components, as well as check pressures and charge refrigerating units.
A. Active recovery   B. Service Valve   C. Gas   D. Recycle

27. _____ Tubing used in refrigeration which has ends to keep tubing clean and dry.
A. Evaporator   B. Joule   C. Refrigerant   D. ACR Tubing

28. _____ Undesirable component in many refrigeration lubricants, which may separate out of solution if cooled sufficiently.
A. Vacuum Pump   B. Red   C. Activated Alumina   D. Wax

29. _____ Any products that are fully manufactured, charged, and hermetically sealed in a factory with five pounds or less of refrigerant
A. Small appliance   B. Farad   C. Active recovery   D. Accumulator

30. _____ A solution or surface that is capable of soaking up (taking in) another substance or energy form.
A. Saddle Valve   B. Absorber   C. Absolute Temperature   D. Piston

31. _____ Light provided with test leads, used to test or probe electrical circuits to determine if they are alive.
A. Effusion   B. Test Light   C. Static Head   D. Calibrate

32. _____ An instrument for measuring resistance in ohms.
A. Storage cylinders   B. Piston Displacement   C. Absolute Zero Temperature   D. Ohmmeter

33. _____ A law stating that the volume of a Gas at a given temperature varies inversely with the applied pressure.
A. Fractionation   B. Decibel   C. Absolute Humidity   D. Boyles Law

34. _____ Pressure operated control which opens electrical circuit if high side pressure becomes excessive.
A. Expansion device   B. Head Pressure Control   C. Evaporator   D. Decibel

35. _____ The temperature rise within an evaporator or suction line assembly from the evaporator's saturation temperature.
A. Super Heat   B. Recover   C. Azeotroph   D. Joule

36. _____ Fluid opening
A. Back Pressure   B. Leak Rate   C. Pressure   D. Back Seating

37. ___ To remove water from a system.
A. Recycle   B. Absolute Zero Temperature   C. Fan   D. Dehydrate

38. ___ Instrument to measuring pressure of gases and vapors.
A. Manometer   B. Adsorption   C. Accumulator   D. Activated Carbon

39. ___ A mechanism that removes flash gas from the evaporator.
A. Econimizer   B. Very high pressure   C. Dew Point   D. Ductwork

40. ___ Chemical compound which is used as a drying agent or desiccant in liquid line filter dryers.
A. Calcium Sulfate   B. Nitrogen   C. Ebulator   D. Manometer

41. ___ Invisible energy caused by the motion of molecules within any substance or matter.
A. Accumulator   B. Head Pressure Control   C. Solenoid Valve   D. Heat

42. ___ Invisible, odorless, and tasteless mixture of gases which form earth's atmosphere.
A. Air   B. Gas   C. Metering Device   D. Ebulator

43. ___ Device or instrument such as a halide torch, an electronic sniffer; or soap solution used to detect leaks.
A. Leak Detector   B. Service Valve   C. Ductwork   D. Partial Pressure

44. ___ Requires the assistance of components such as the appliance or unit's compressor to remove the refrigerant from the appliance.
A. Evaporator Coil   B. Psychrometer   C. Passive recovery   D. Mixture

45. ___ cause to be or remain alone or apart from others.
A. Halide Refrigerants   B. Isolate   C. Capacitance   D. Chlorine

46. ___ To extract refrigerant from an appliance and clean refrigerant for reuse without meeting all of the requirements for reclamation.
A. Recycle   B. Dew Point   C. Actuator   D. Ebulator

47. ___ Any person who performs maintenance, service, or repair that could reasonably be expected to release class I or class II substances into the atmosphere.
A. Evaporator Coil   B. Leak Detector   C. Opening   D. Technician

48. ___ Storage tank which receives liquid refrigerant from evaporator and prevents it from flowing into suction line.
A. Head Pressure Control   B. Accumulator   C. Static Head   D. Absolute Humidity

49. ___ Pressure of fluid expressed in terms of height of column of the fluid, such as water or mercury.
A. Absolute Humidity   B. Static Head   C. Test Light   D. Pascals Law

50. ___ Converting recycled refrigerant into a product to be reused.
A. Pressure   B. Partial Pressure   C. Reclaim   D. OHM

51. ___ The temperature at which the non-azeotropic blend first begins to evaporate.
A. Manometer   B. Bubble Point   C. Refrigerant   D. Filter

52. ___ Temperature measured from absolute zero.
A. Absolute Temperature   B. Dehydrate   C. Metering Device   D. Fractionation

53. ___ Forming a homogeneous mixture of liquids when added together.
A. Hydrocarbon   B. PSC Motor   C. Miscible   D. Ohmmeter

54. ___ Vapor phase or state of a substance.
A. Safety Plug   B. Hydrostatic   C. Gas   D. Bubble Point

55. ___ Instrument used to measure pressures below atmospheric pressure.
A. Vacuum Gauge   B. Evacuation   C. Ohms Law   D. Head Pressure

56. _____ A passive throttling device, comprised of a small opening, located upstream of the evaporator.
A. Ebulator   B. Boyles Law   C. Zeotropic   D. Orifice Plate

57. _____ A mixture of at least two different liquids.
A. Isomer   B. Zeotropic   C. Azeotroph   D. Distillation

58. _____ A refrigerant has a boiling point between minus 50C and 10C degrees at atmospheric pressure.
A. Ebulator   B. High pressure   C. ACR Tubing   D. Limit Control

59. _____ The heart or "pump" within an air conditioning or heat pump system.
A. Refrigerant circuit   B. TON   C. Junction Box   D. Compressor

60. _____ Type of torch used to detect halogen refrigerant leaks.
A. Refrigerant   B. Halide Torch   C. Capacitance   D. De Minimus

61. _____ A sensation felt as a result of the absence of heat.
A. Refrigeration   B. Absolute Temperature   C. Cold   D. Safety Plug

62. _____ Pressure which exists in condensing side of refrigerating system.
A. Vacuum Gauge   B. Off Cycle   C. Pinch off Tool   D. Head Pressure

63. _____ Close fitting part which moves up and down in a cylinder.
A. Piston   B. Partial Pressure   C. Boyles Law   D. Distillation

64. _____ The process in which a gas flows through a small hole in a container.
A. Line Set   B. Absolute Humidity   C. Blue   D. Effusion

65. _____ Valve actuated by magnetic action by means of an electrically energized coil.
A. Parallel   B. British Thermal Unit   C. Zeotropic   D. Solenoid Valve

66. _____ Treaty among nations designed to protect the stratospheric ozone layer.
A. Orifice Plate   B. Ohms Law   C. Montreal Protocol   D. Field Pole

67. _____ The parts of an appliance that are normally connected to each other and are designed to contain refrigerant.
A. Refrigerant circuit   B. Kilometer   C. Micron   D. Junction Box

68. _____ Electrical "pressure" applied to a circuit.
A. Capacitance   B. Volt   C. Service Valve   D. Fractionation

69. _____ Degree of hotness or coldness as measured by a thermometer
A. Range   B. Temperature   C. Eddy Currents   D. Accumulator

70. _____ Equipment that has its own compressor or pump.
A. Compound gauge   B. Very high pressure   C. PSC Motor   D. Active recovery

71. _____ Round or rectangular pipes or controlled paths acting as conduit for return, mixed, makeup, supply or exhaust air.
A. Activated Carbon   B. Ductwork   C. Econimizer   D. Charles Law

72. _____ One of a group of substances having the same combination of elements but arranged spatially in different ways.
A. Halide Torch   B. Wax   C. Recycle   D. Isomer

73. _____ Reducing contaminants in the used refrigerant
A. Kelvin   B. Recycle   C. Center port   D. Humidity

74. _____ Electrical device used to open circuit if the temperature, pressure, and
A. Zeotropic   B. Opening   C. ACR Tubing   D. Safety Motor Control

75. _____ Need to evacuate system to eliminate air and moisture at the end of service.
A. Dehydration Evacuation   B. Disposable cylinders   C. Damper   D. Fractionation

76. _____ Gray cylinder with a yellow top; used for recovery or transporting refrigerant.
A. Vacuum Gauge   B. Kelvin   C. Reusable cylinders   D. Field Pole

77. _____ Control used to open or close electrical circuits as temperature or pressure limits are reached.
A. Ohms Law   B. Gauge manifold   C. Limit Control   D. Condenser

78. _____ Latin for the least amount of Refrigerant you can release into the atmosphere.
A. Service Manifold   B. Back Pressure   C. Cold   D. De Minimus

79. _____ The moving of heat from an undesirable location, to that of a location where its presence is less undesirable.
A. Gas   B. Dehydrate   C. Refrigeration   D. Absolute Pressure

80. _____ High Pressure
A. Orifice Plate   B. Blue   C. Red   D. PSC Motor

81. _____ Pressure in low side of refrigerating system; also called suction pressure or low side pressure.
A. Heat   B. Back Pressure   C. Accumulator   D. Zeotropic

82. _____ Heat energy absorbed in process of changing form of substance without change in temperature or pressure.
A. Service Valve   B. Latent Heat   C. Expansion device   D. Red

83. _____ Refrigerator which creates low temperatures by using the cooling effect formed when a refrigerant is absorbed by chemical substance.
A. Disposable cylinders   B. Absorption Refrigerator   C. Atmosphere   D. Low pressure

84. _____ Unit of electrical capacity; capacity of a condenser which, when charged with one coulomb of electricity, gives difference of potential of one volt.
A. Azeotroph   B. Farad   C. Condenser Coil   D. Vapor

85. _____ The total amount of moisture in air.
A. Cold   B. Absolute Humidity   C. Humidity   D. Piston Displacement

86. _____ That portion of a regulating valve that converts mechanical fluid, thermal energy, or electrical energy into mechanical motion to open or close valve seats.
A. Accumulator   B. Accelerate   C. Blue   D. Actuator

87. _____ A form of testing for high pressure cylinders.
A. Compressor   B. Halon   C. Joule   D. Hydrostatic

88. _____ Property of non-conductor that permits storage of electrical energy in an electrostatic field.
A. Field Pole   B. Fractionation   C. Super Heat   D. Capacitance

89. _____ To remove refrigerant in any condition from an appliance and store it in an external container without necessarily testing or processing it in any way.
A. Absolute Temperature   B. Calcium Sulfate   C. Acid Condition   D. Recover

90. _____ The fluid used for heat transfer in a refrigeration system, which absorbs heat during evaporation at low temperature and pressure, and releases heat during condensation.
A. Purge unit   B. Refrigerant   C. Density   D. Dew Point

91. _____ Gas used for leak detection.
A. Nitrogen   B. Gas   C. Range   D. Off Cycle

92. _____ One thousandth of a millimeter.
A. Accelerate   B. Joule   C. PSC Motor   D. Micron

93. _____ Substance with ability to take up, or absorb another substance.
A. Partial Pressure   B. Absorbent   C. Absolute Zero Temperature   D. Very high pressure

94. _____ Converts high pressure liquid to low pressure vapor
A. Absorber   B. Expansion device   C. Junction Box   D. Orifice Plate

95. _____ A pointed or sharp edged solid substance inserted in flooded type evaporators to improve evaporation (boiling) of refrigerant in coil.
A. Head Pressure   B. Refrigeration   C. Ebulator   D. Absorbent

96. _____ Any device which contains a refrigerant and which is used for household or commercial purposes, including any air conditioner, refrigerator, chiller, or freezer.
A. Evaporator   B. Adiabatic Compression   C. Calorimeter   D. Appliance

97. _____ The process of cooling or chilling.
A. Receiver Heating Element   B. Refrigeration   C. Decibel   D. Filter

98. _____ A substance produces a refrigerating or cooling effect while expanding or vaporizing.
A. Refrigerant   B. Farad   C. Pressure   D. Calcium Sulfate

99. _____ A standard unit of measure for electrical resistance.
A. Recycle   B. OHM   C. Refrigerant   D. Test Light

100. _____ Device which releases the contents of a container above normal pressures, and before rupture pressures are reached.
A. Filter   B. Safety Plug   C. Kelvin   D. Dehydration Evacuation

B. From the words provided for each clue, provide the letter of the word which best matches the clue.

1. _____ The parts of an appliance that are normally connected to each other and are designed to contain refrigerant.
A. Rupture disc   B. Absolute Humidity   C. Refrigerant circuit   D. Dew Point

2. _____ A refrigerant has a boiling point above 10C or 50F at atmospheric pressure.
A. Vacuum Gauge   B. Disposable cylinders   C. Joule   D. Low pressure

3. _____ A temperature control device. Typically mounted in conditioned space.
A. Halide Refrigerants   B. Thermostat   C. Junction Box   D. Piston Displacement

4. _____ Control used to open or close electrical circuits as temperature or pressure limits are reached.
A. Limit Control   B. Rupture disc   C. Kelvin   D. Boyles Law

5. _____ Typically, a multi ported valve used by service technicians to isolate remote system components, as well as check pressures and charge refrigerating units.
A. ACR Tubing   B. Service Valve   C. Montreal Protocol   D. Dew Point

6. _____ A substance formed by a union of two or more elements
A. Absolute Pressure   B. Compound   C. Evaporator   D. Decibel

7. _____ Valve actuated by magnetic action by means of an electrically energized coil.
A. Solenoid Valve   B. Range   C. Dew Point   D. Vacuum Control System

8. _____ A device equipped with gauges and manual valves, used by serviceman to service refrigerating systems.
A. Gas   B. Therm   C. Service Manifold   D. Eddy Currents

9. _____ A pressure imposed upon a fluid is transmitted equally in all directions.
A. Absorber   B. Induction Motor   C. Disposable cylinders   D. Pascals Law

10. _____ Device or instrument such as a halide torch, an electronic sniffer; or soap solution used to detect leaks.
A. Vacuum Pump   B. Calorimeter   C. Storage cylinders   D. Leak Detector

11. _____ Converts high pressure liquid to low pressure vapor
A. Adsorption   B. Expansion device   C. Appliance   D. Pinch off Tool

12. _____ The temperature at which the non-azeotropic blend first begins to condense.
A. Density   B. Farad   C. Dew Point   D. Absorbent

13. _____ A chemical used in fire extinguishing.
A. Atmosphere   B. Halon   C. ACR Tubing   D. Latent Heat

14. _____ Invisible energy caused by the motion of molecules within any substance or matter.
A. Heat   B. Junction Box   C. Velocity Head   D. Evaporator Coil

15. _____ To determine; position indicators as required to obtain accurate measurements.
A. Temperature Glide   B. Pascals Law   C. Calibrate   D. Junction Box

16. _____ To remove refrigerant in any condition from an appliance and store it in an external container without necessarily testing or processing it in any way.
A. Recover   B. Joule   C. Calibrate   D. Storage cylinders

17. _____ Part of stator of motor which concentrates magnetic field of field winding.
A. Field Pole   B. Pressure   C. Refrigeration   D. Gas

18. _____ A passive throttling device, comprised of a small opening, located upstream of the evaporator.
A. Orifice Plate   B. Capacitance   C. Evaporator   D. Isomer

19. _____ An independent refrigeration system that separates the non-condensables from the refrigerant and re-condenses and collects any refrigerant in the exhaust vent stream.
A. Saddle Valve   B. Purge unit   C. Distillation   D. Heat Exchanger

20. _____ Instrument used to measure pressures below atmospheric pressure.
A. Vacuum Gauge   B. Damper   C. Pinch off Tool   D. Fractionation

21. _____ High Pressure
A. Mixture   B. Orifice Plate   C. Red   D. Temperature

22. _____ Unit of electrical power, equal to 1000 watts.
A. Econimizer   B. Therm   C. Evaporator Coil   D. Kilometer

23. _____ The piping used to connect the outdoor unit to the indoor unit.
A. Saddle Valve   B. Line Set   C. Field Pole   D. Absorbent

24. _____ The process of extracting any air, non-condensable gases, or water from the system.
A. Evacuation   B. Montreal Protocol   C. Absorbent   D. Recycle

25. _____ Substance used to counteract acids, in refrigeration system.
A. Dehydrate   B. Vacuum   C. Absorption Chiller   D. Neutralizer

26. _____ Unit of measure referring to the flow of electrons within a circuit.
A. Ampere   B. Fan   C. Eddy Currents   D. Chlorine

27. _____ The process in which a gas flows through a small hole in a container.
A. Temperature Glide   B. Micron   C. Absolute Zero Temperature   D. Effusion

28. _____ Heat energy absorbed in process of changing form of substance without change in temperature or pressure.
A. Neutralizer   B. Ohms Law   C. Refrigeration   D. Latent Heat

29. _____ Compressing refrigerant gas without removing or adding heat.
A. Small appliance   B. Heat   C. Adiabatic Compression   D. Insulation

30. _____ Creates pressure drop to allow liquid refrigerant to boil and absorb latent heat.
A. Metering Device   B. Boyles Law   C. De Minimus   D. Low pressure

31. _____ An AC motor which operates on principle of rotating magnetic field. Rotor has no electrical connection, but receives electrical energy by transformer action from field windings.
A. Induction Motor   B. Air   C. Zeotropic   D. Ohmmeter

32. _____ Any material or substance which has the ability to retard the flow or transfer of heat.
A. Ohms Law   B. Saddle Valve   C. OHM   D. Insulation

33. _____ Light provided with test leads, used to test or probe electrical circuits to determine if they are alive.
A. Test Light   B. Halide Torch   C. Adsorbent   D. Refrigerant

34. _____ protects equipment or system from over pressurization or damaging vacuum conditions.
A. Rupture disc   B. Accumulator   C. Absorber   D. Latent Heat

35. _____ A law stating that the volume of a Gas at a given temperature varies inversely with the applied pressure.
A. Boyles Law   B. Actuator   C. Metering Device   D. Psychrometer

36. _____ Accumulates any low pressure liquid from the evaporator so it can vaporize before entering the compressor
A. Activated Carbon   B. OHM   C. Latent Heat   D. Accumulator

37. _____ A mixture of at least two different liquids.
A. Latent Heat   B. Head Pressure   C. Azeotroph   D. Actuator

38. _____ Side by side and having the same distance continuously between them.
A. Latent Heat   B. Parallel   C. Halon   D. Induction Motor

39. _____ Condition in which refrigerant and
A. Accelerate   B. Calibrate   C. Acid Condition   D. Activated Alumina

40. _____ Electrical resistance mounted in or around liquid receiver, used to maintain head pressures when ambient temperature is at freezing or below freezing.
A. Thermostat   B. Kelvin   C. Receiver Heating Element   D. Adiabatic Compression

41. _____ Round or rectangular pipes or controlled paths acting as conduit for return, mixed, makeup, supply or exhaust air.
A. Ductwork   B. Bubble Point   C. Density   D. Refrigerant

42. _____ High-efficiency design motor used on virtually all of today's HVAC & R equipment requiring motors.
A. Isolate   B. PSC Motor   C. Limit Control   D. Hydrostatic

43. _____ States that the volume occupied by a gas at a constant Pressure is directly proportional to the absolute temperature.
A. Compound   B. Charles Law   C. Halide Refrigerants   D. Off Cycle

44. _____ Gauge pressure plus atmospheric pressure (14.7 lbs. per sq. in.).
A. Absolute Pressure   B. Actuator   C. Compressor   D. High pressure

45. _____ One thousandth of a millimeter.
A. Joule   B. Fan   C. Manometer   D. Micron

46. _____ The process of collecting used refrigerant.
A. Recover   B. De Minimus   C. Service Valve   D. Recovery

47. _____ The SI base unit of temperature; a unit on an absolute temperature scale.
A. Opening   B. Super Heat   C. Reclaim   D. Kelvin

48. _____ A substance produces a refrigerating or cooling effect while expanding or vaporizing.
A. British Thermal Unit   B. Watt   C. Refrigerant   D. Recover

49. _____ That time period of a refrigeration cycle when the system is not operating.
A. Ampere   B. Storage cylinders   C. Off Cycle   D. Small appliance

50. _____ Either a sling type, or electronic. Instrument used to determine wet bulb temperatures and relative humidity.
A. Micron   B. Temperature Glide   C. Saturation Temperature   D. Psychrometer

51. _____ Tubing used in refrigeration which has ends to keep tubing clean and dry.
A. Humidity   B. Blue   C. Halon   D. ACR Tubing

52. _____ The form of matter that is an easily compressible fluid
A. Temperature   B. Gas   C. Accumulator   D. Volt

53. _____ Substance with ability to take up, or absorb another substance.
A. Absorbent   B. Service Manifold   C. Humidity   D. Vacuum

54. _____ Device used to measure quantities of heat or determine specific heats.
A. Thermostat   B. Accelerate   C. Vacuum   D. Calorimeter

55. _____ Receives high pressure liquid from the condenser
A. Red   B. Therm   C. Receiver   D. Leak Detector

56. _____ The process of cooling or chilling.
A. Absolute Pressure   B. Disposable cylinders   C. Volt   D. Refrigeration

57. _____ To remove water from a system.
A. Field Pole   B. Ultraviolet Radiation   C. Eddy Currents   D. Dehydrate

58. _____ The moving of heat from an undesirable location, to that of a location where its presence is less undesirable.
A. Piston Displacement   B. Refrigeration   C. Volt   D. Montreal Protocol

59. _____ Pressure in low side of refrigerating system; also called suction pressure or low side pressure.
A. Chlorine   B. Back Pressure   C. Reusable cylinders   D. Service Manifold

60. _____ Evaporates low pressure vapor from the expansion device
A. Vapor   B. Safety Plug   C. Farad   D. Evaporator

61. _____ A radial or axial flow device used for moving or producing artificial currents of air.
A. Metering Device   B. Acid Condition   C. Fan   D. Humidity

62. _____ A compound containing only the elements hydrogen and carbon.
A. Safety Motor Control   B. Heat Exchanger   C. Adsorption   D. Hydrocarbon

63. _____ Single use cylinders. Empty cylinders should have the pressure reduced to zero and the cylinder rendered unusable.
A. Chlorine   B. Activated Alumina   C. Head Pressure   D. Disposable cylinders

64. _____ Induced currents flowing in a core.
A. Accumulator   B. Eddy Currents   C. Vacuum Gauge   D. Ohmmeter

65. _____ Each refrigerant in the blend keeps its own temperature and pressure characteristics.
A. Vacuum   B. Zeotropic   C. Damper   D. Fan

66. _____ A form of testing for high pressure cylinders.
A. Recovery   B. Refrigeration   C. Hydrostatic   D. Isomer

67. _____ Any products that are fully manufactured, charged, and hermetically sealed in a factory with five pounds or less of refrigerant
A. Metering Device   B. Small appliance   C. Center port   D. Effusion

68. _____ Reduction in pressure below atmospheric pressure.
A. Adsorbent   B. Compressor   C. Vacuum   D. Back Seating

69. _____ Mathematical relationships between voltage, current and resistance in an electric circuit, discovered by George Simon Ohm.
A. Leak Rate   B. Chlorine   C. Diffusion   D. Ohms Law

70. _____ The action of purifying a liquid by a process of heating and cooling.
A. De Minimus   B. Vapor   C. Distillation   D. Absolute Humidity

71. _____ The total amount of moisture in air.
A. Air   B. Leak Detector   C. Humidity   D. Compound

72. _____ To extract refrigerant from an appliance and clean refrigerant for reuse without meeting all of the requirements for reclamation.
A. Kelvin   B. Technician   C. Recycle   D. Vacuum

73. _____ Any maintenance or repair on an appliance that would release refrigerant from the appliance to the atmosphere.
A. Opening   B. Orifice Plate   C. Actuator   D. Refrigerant

74. _____ Group of electrical terminals housed in protective box or container.
A. Junction Box   B. Micron   C. Ebulator   D. Heat

75. _____ Instrument to measuring pressure of gases and vapors.
A. Opening   B. Recycle   C. Off Cycle   D. Manometer

76. _____ The difference between the Dew Point and the Bubble Point.
A. Storage cylinders   B. Temperature Glide   C. Adiabatic Compression   D. Absorber

77. _____ Requires the assistance of components such as the appliance or unit's compressor to remove the refrigerant from the appliance.
A. Vacuum Gauge   B. Passive recovery   C. Flame Test   D. Activated Carbon

78. _____ Unit of electrical capacity; capacity of a condenser which, when charged with one coulomb of electricity, gives difference of potential of one volt.
A. Montreal Protocol   B. Boyles Law   C. Farad   D. Psychrometer

79. _____ Any person who performs maintenance, service, or repair that could reasonably be expected to release class I or class II substances into the atmosphere.
A. Absorbent   B. Recycle   C. Absolute Humidity   D. Technician

80. _____ The process whereby a gas spreads out through another gas to occupy the space with uniform partial Pressure.
A. Micron   B. Orifice Plate   C. Diffusion   D. Chlorine

81. _____ Latin for the least amount of Refrigerant you can release into the atmosphere.
A. Volt   B. De Minimus   C. Activated Alumina   D. Compound gauge

82. _____ The force exerted per unit area of surface.
A. Halide Torch   B. Ohms Law   C. Pressure   D. Junction Box

83. _____ Tool which is principally a torch and when an air refrigerant mixture is fed to flame, this flame will change color in presence of heated copper.
A. Montreal Protocol   B. Ozone layer   C. Mixture   D. Flame Test

84. _____ A standard unit of measure for electrical resistance.
A. Red   B. Micron   C. Range   D. OHM

85.   The temperature at which the non-azeotropic blend first begins to evaporate.
A. Bubble Point   B. Absolute Pressure   C. Ultraviolet Radiation   D. Volt

86.   Special high efficiency device (pump) used create deep vacuum within an AC
A. Service Valve   B. Vacuum Pump   C. Absolute Humidity   D. Fan

87.   Unit of electrical power.
A. Montreal Protocol   B. Safety Motor Control   C. Fractionation   D. Watt

88.   Need to evacuate system to eliminate air and moisture at the end of service.
A. Therm   B. Hydrostatic   C. Orifice Plate   D. Dehydration Evacuation

89.   Pressure of fluid expressed in terms of height of column of the fluid, such as water or mercury.
A. Range   B. Orifice Plate   C. Absorbent   D. Static Head

90.   A tool that measures pressure readings at different points in the refrigeration system.
A. Back Pressure   B. Low pressure   C. Gauge manifold   D. Back Seating

91.   Vapor phase or state of a substance.
A. Gas   B. Small appliance   C. Hydrostatic   D. Effusion

92.   Device for removing small particles from a fluid.
A. Halide Torch   B. Evaporator   C. Purge unit   D. Filter

93.   Pressure or temperature settings of a control; change within limits.
A. Range   B. Fractionation   C. Thermostat   D. Miscible

94.   Converting recycled refrigerant into a product to be reused.
A. Metering Device   B. Density   C. Reclaim   D. Diffusion

95.   The Gaseous state of any kind of matter that normally exists as a liquid or solid.
A. Absolute Temperature   B. Safety Control   C. Pinch off Tool   D. Vapor

96.   Measures low pressure and vacuum.
A. Absorbent   B. Disposable cylinders   C. Vacuum Control System   D. Compound gauge

97.   A blend of two or more components that do not a have fixed proportion to one another.
A. Junction Box   B. Damper   C. Mixture   D. Diffusion

98.   Any device which contains a refrigerant and which is used for household or commercial purposes, including any air conditioner, refrigerator, chiller, or freezer.
A. Center port   B. Limit Control   C. Vacuum Pump   D. Appliance

99.   Amount of moisture in the air, indicated in grains per cubic foot.
A. Bubble Point   B. Absolute Humidity   C. Recover   D. Storage cylinders

100.   The temperature where a refrigerant exists in both liquid and vapor form relative to its measured pressure.
A. Wet Bulb   B. Absorption Chiller   C. Saturation Temperature   D. Pressure

A. From the words provided for each clue, provide the letter of the word which best matches the clue.

1. _A_ A refrigerant has a boiling point below minus 50C or minus 58F at atmospheric pressure.
   A. Very high pressure   B. Passive recovery   C. Micron   D. Volt

2. _C_ The temperature where a refrigerant exists in both liquid and vapor form relative to its measured pressure.
   A. Compound gauge   B. Diffusion   C. Saturation Temperature   D. Vacuum Pump

3. _D_ Part of stator of motor which concentrates magnetic field of field winding.
   A. Isomer   B. Acid Condition   C. Absolute Pressure   D. Field Pole

4. _B_ Quantity of heat equivalent to 100,000 Btu.
   A. Kelvin   B. Therm   C. Safety Control   D. OHM

5. _C_ Temperature at which molecular motion ceases.
   A. Evaporator Coil   B. Vacuum Gauge   C. Absolute Zero Temperature   D. Calcium Sulfate

6. _D_ The piping used to connect the outdoor unit to the indoor unit.
   A. Purge unit   B. Evacuation   C. Absolute Humidity   D. Line Set

7. _C_ A substance formed by a union of two or more elements
   A. Heat Exchanger   B. Heat   C. Compound   D. Expansion device

8. _D_ Condenses high pressure gas from the compressor to high pressure liquid.
   A. Diffusion   B. Activated Carbon   C. Distillation   D. Condenser

9. _C_ Gauge pressure plus atmospheric pressure (14.7 lbs. per sq. in.).
   A. Service Manifold   B. Solenoid Valve   C. Absolute Pressure   D. Farad

10. _D_ High-efficiency design motor used on virtually all of today's HVAC & R equipment requiring motors.
    A. Gas   B. Off Cycle   C. Pinch off Tool   D. PSC Motor

11. _C_ Measures low pressure and vacuum.
    A. Calorimeter   B. Miscible   C. Compound gauge   D. Absolute Temperature

12. _B_ Represents the amount of energy required to raise one pound of water one degree Fahrenheit.
    A. Recovery   B. British Thermal Unit   C. Halide Refrigerants   D. Fan

13. _B_ Pressure or temperature settings of a control; change within limits.
    A. ACR Tubing   B. Range   C. Pascals Law   D. Service Valve

14. _D_ Device used to press walls of a tubing together until fluid flow ceases.
    A. Gauge manifold   B. King Valve   C. Appliance   D. Pinch off Tool

15. _B_ The action of purifying a liquid by a process of heating and cooling.
    A. Isolate   B. Distillation   C. Appliance   D. Heat Exchanger

16. _C_ Condition in which refrigerant and
    A. Refrigeration   B. Therm   C. Acid Condition   D. Parallel

17. _D_ Accumulates any low pressure liquid from the evaporator so it can vaporize before entering the compressor
    A. Temperature   B. Calibrate   C. Adsorbent   D. Accumulator

18. _D_ Where heat is absorbed by warm air passing across. Liquid refrigerant boils as it is metered into coil, and changes from liquid to vapor.
    A. Partial Pressure   B. Isolate   C. Insulation   D. Evaporator Coil

19. __B__ A device equipped with gauges and manual valves, used by serviceman to service refrigerating systems.
A. Absorbent   B. Service Manifold   C. Adsorption   D. De Minimus

20. __C__ Dissipates heat from the refrigerant.
A. Temperature Glide   B. Diffusion   C. Condenser Coil   D. Receiver

21. __A__ Creates pressure drop to allow liquid refrigerant to boil and absorb latent heat.
A. Metering Device   B. Latent Heat   C. Ampere   D. Sub Cooling

22. __B__ Device used in measurement of relative humidity. Evaporation of moisture lowers temperature of wet bulb compared to dry bulb temperature in same area.
A. Boyles Law   B. Wet Bulb   C. Joule   D. Receiver Heating Element

23. __B__ In flowing fluid, height of fluid equivalent to its velocity pressure.
A. Saddle Valve   B. Velocity Head   C. Center port   D. Ohmmeter

24. __D__ Tool which is principally a torch and when an air refrigerant mixture is fed to flame, this flame will change color in presence of heated copper.
A. Dehydrate   B. Volt   C. High pressure   D. Flame Test

25. __C__ Special high efficiency device (pump) used create deep vacuum within an AC
A. Vapor   B. Zeotropic   C. Vacuum Pump   D. Kilometer

26. __B__ Typically, a multi ported valve used by service technicians to isolate remote system components, as well as check pressures and charge refrigerating units.
A. Active recovery   B. Service Valve   C. Gas   D. Recycle

27. __D__ Tubing used in refrigeration which has ends to keep tubing clean and dry.
A. Evaporator   B. Joule   C. Refrigerant   D. ACR Tubing

28. __D__ Undesirable component in many refrigeration lubricants, which may separate out of solution if cooled sufficiently.
A. Vacuum Pump   B. Red   C. Activated Alumina   D. Wax

29. __A__ Any products that are fully manufactured, charged, and hermetically sealed in a factory with five pounds or less of refrigerant
A. Small appliance   B. Farad   C. Active recovery   D. Accumulator

30. __B__ A solution or surface that is capable of soaking up (taking in) another substance or energy form.
A. Saddle Valve   B. Absorber   C. Absolute Temperature   D. Piston

31. __B__ Light provided with test leads, used to test or probe electrical circuits to determine if they are alive.
A. Effusion   B. Test Light   C. Static Head   D. Calibrate

32. __D__ An instrument for measuring resistance in ohms.
A. Storage cylinders   B. Piston Displacement   C. Absolute Zero Temperature   D. Ohmmeter

33. __D__ A law stating that the volume of a Gas at a given temperature varies inversely with the applied pressure.
A. Fractionation   B. Decibel   C. Absolute Humidity   D. Boyles Law

34. __B__ Pressure operated control which opens electrical circuit if high side pressure becomes excessive.
A. Expansion device   B. Head Pressure Control   C. Evaporator   D. Decibel

35. __A__ The temperature rise within an evaporator or suction line assembly from the evaporator's saturation temperature.
A. Super Heat   B. Recover   C. Azeotroph   D. Joule

36. __D__ Fluid opening
A. Back Pressure   B. Leak Rate   C. Pressure   D. Back Seating

37. __D__ To remove water from a system.
A. Recycle   B. Absolute Zero Temperature   C. Fan   D. Dehydrate

38. __A__ Instrument to measuring pressure of gases and vapors.
A. Manometer   B. Adsorption   C. Accumulator   D. Activated Carbon

39. __A__ A mechanism that removes flash gas from the evaporator.
A. Econimizer   B. Very high pressure   C. Dew Point   D. Ductwork

40. __A__ Chemical compound which is used as a drying agent or desiccant in liquid line filter dryers.
A. Calcium Sulfate   B. Nitrogen   C. Ebulator   D. Manometer

41. __D__ Invisible energy caused by the motion of molecules within any substance or matter.
A. Accumulator   B. Head Pressure Control   C. Solenoid Valve   D. Heat

42. __A__ Invisible, odorless, and tasteless mixture of gases which form earth's atmosphere.
A. Air   B. Gas   C. Metering Device   D. Ebulator

43. __A__ Device or instrument such as a halide torch, an electronic sniffer; or soap solution used to detect leaks.
A. Leak Detector   B. Service Valve   C. Ductwork   D. Partial Pressure

44. __C__ Requires the assistance of components such as the appliance or unit's compressor to remove the refrigerant from the appliance.
A. Evaporator Coil   B. Psychrometer   C. Passive recovery   D. Mixture

45. __B__ cause to be or remain alone or apart from others.
A. Halide Refrigerants   B. Isolate   C. Capacitance   D. Chlorine

46. __A__ To extract refrigerant from an appliance and clean refrigerant for reuse without meeting all of the requirements for reclamation.
A. Recycle   B. Dew Point   C. Actuator   D. Ebulator

47. __D__ Any person who performs maintenance, service, or repair that could reasonably be expected to release class I or class II substances into the atmosphere.
A. Evaporator Coil   B. Leak Detector   C. Opening   D. Technician

48. __B__ Storage tank which receives liquid refrigerant from evaporator and prevents it from flowing into suction line.
A. Head Pressure Control   B. Accumulator   C. Static Head   D. Absolute Humidity

49. __B__ Pressure of fluid expressed in terms of height of column of the fluid, such as water or mercury.
A. Absolute Humidity   B. Static Head   C. Test Light   D. Pascals Law

50. __C__ Converting recycled refrigerant into a product to be reused.
A. Pressure   B. Partial Pressure   C. Reclaim   D. OHM

51. __B__ The temperature at which the non-azeotropic blend first begins to evaporate.
A. Manometer   B. Bubble Point   C. Refrigerant   D. Filter

52. __A__ Temperature measured from absolute zero.
A. Absolute Temperature   B. Dehydrate   C. Metering Device   D. Fractionation

53. __C__ Forming a homogeneous mixture of liquids when added together.
A. Hydrocarbon   B. PSC Motor   C. Miscible   D. Ohmmeter

54. __C__ Vapor phase or state of a substance.
A. Safety Plug   B. Hydrostatic   C. Gas   D. Bubble Point

55. __A__ Instrument used to measure pressures below atmospheric pressure.
A. Vacuum Gauge   B. Evacuation   C. Ohms Law   D. Head Pressure

56. D A passive throttling device, comprised of a small opening, located upstream of the evaporator.
    A. Ebulator B. Boyles Law C. Zeotropic D. Orifice Plate

57. C A mixture of at least two different liquids.
    A. Isomer B. Zeotropic C. Azeotroph D. Distillation

58. B A refrigerant has a boiling point between minus 50C and 10C degrees at atmospheric pressure.
    A. Ebulator B. High pressure C. ACR Tubing D. Limit Control

59. D The heart or "pump" within an air conditioning or heat pump system.
    A. Refrigerant circuit B. TON C. Junction Box D. Compressor

60. B Type of torch used to detect halogen refrigerant leaks.
    A. Refrigerant B. Halide Torch C. Capacitance D. De Minimus

61. C A sensation felt as a result of the absence of heat.
    A. Refrigeration B. Absolute Temperature C. Cold D. Safety Plug

62. D Pressure which exists in condensing side of refrigerating system.
    A. Vacuum Gauge B. Off Cycle C. Pinch off Tool D. Head Pressure

63. A Close fitting part which moves up and down in a cylinder.
    A. Piston B. Partial Pressure C. Boyles Law D. Distillation

64. D The process in which a gas flows through a small hole in a container.
    A. Line Set B. Absolute Humidity C. Blue D. Effusion

65. D Valve actuated by magnetic action by means of an electrically energized coil.
    A. Parallel B. British Thermal Unit C. Zeotropic D. Solenoid Valve

66. C Treaty among nations designed to protect the stratospheric ozone layer.
    A. Orifice Plate B. Ohms Law C. Montreal Protocol D. Field Pole

67. A The parts of an appliance that are normally connected to each other and are designed to contain refrigerant.
    A. Refrigerant circuit B. Kilometer C. Micron D. Junction Box

68. B Electrical "pressure" applied to a circuit.
    A. Capacitance B. Volt C. Service Valve D. Fractionation

69. B Degree of hotness or coldness as measured by a thermometer
    A. Range B. Temperature C. Eddy Currents D. Accumulator

70. D Equipment that has its own compressor or pump.
    A. Compound gauge B. Very high pressure C. PSC Motor D. Active recovery

71. B Round or rectangular pipes or controlled paths acting as conduit for return, mixed, makeup, supply or exhaust air.
    A. Activated Carbon B. Ductwork C. Econimizer D. Charles Law

72. D One of a group of substances having the same combination of elements but arranged spatially in different ways.
    A. Halide Torch B. Wax C. Recycle D. Isomer

73. B Reducing contaminants in the used refrigerant
    A. Kelvin B. Recycle C. Center port D. Humidity

74. D Electrical device used to open circuit if the temperature, pressure, and
    A. Zeotropic B. Opening C. ACR Tubing D. Safety Motor Control

75. A   Need to evacuate system to eliminate air and moisture at the end of service.
A. Dehydration Evacuation   B. Disposable cylinders   C. Damper   D. Fractionation

76. C   Gray cylinder with a yellow top; used for recovery or transporting refrigerant.
A. Vacuum Gauge   B. Kelvin   C. Reusable cylinders   D. Field Pole

77. C   Control used to open or close electrical circuits as temperature or pressure limits are reached.
A. Ohms Law   B. Gauge manifold   C. Limit Control   D. Condenser

78. D   Latin for the least amount of Refrigerant you can release into the atmosphere.
A. Service Manifold   B. Back Pressure   C. Cold   D. De Minimus

79. C   The moving of heat from an undesirable location, to that of a location where its presence is less undesirable.
A. Gas   B. Dehydrate   C. Refrigeration   D. Absolute Pressure

80. C   High Pressure
A. Orifice Plate   B. Blue   C. Red   D. PSC Motor

81. B   Pressure in low side of refrigerating system; also called suction pressure or low side pressure.
A. Heat   B. Back Pressure   C. Accumulator   D. Zeotropic

82. B   Heat energy absorbed in process of changing form of substance without change in temperature or pressure.
A. Service Valve   B. Latent Heat   C. Expansion device   D. Red

83. B   Refrigerator which creates low temperatures by using the cooling effect formed when a refrigerant is absorbed by chemical substance.
A. Disposable cylinders   B. Absorption Refrigerator   C. Atmosphere   D. Low pressure

84. B   Unit of electrical capacity; capacity of a condenser which, when charged with one coulomb of electricity, gives difference of potential of one volt.
A. Azeotroph   B. Farad   C. Condenser Coil   D. Vapor

85. C   The total amount of moisture in air.
A. Cold   B. Absolute Humidity   C. Humidity   D. Piston Displacement

86. D   That portion of a regulating valve that converts mechanical fluid, thermal energy, or electrical energy into mechanical motion to open or close valve seats.
A. Accumulator   B. Accelerate   C. Blue   D. Actuator

87. D   A form of testing for high pressure cylinders.
A. Compressor   B. Halon   C. Joule   D. Hydrostatic

88. D   Property of non-conductor that permits storage of electrical energy in an electrostatic field.
A. Field Pole   B. Fractionation   C. Super Heat   D. Capacitance

89. D   To remove refrigerant in any condition from an appliance and store it in an external container without necessarily testing or processing it in any way.
A. Absolute Temperature   B. Calcium Sulfate   C. Acid Condition   D. Recover

90. B   The fluid used for heat transfer in a refrigeration system, which absorbs heat during evaporation at low temperature and pressure, and releases heat during condensation.
A. Purge unit   B. Refrigerant   C. Density   D. Dew Point

91. A   Gas used for leak detection.
A. Nitrogen   B. Gas   C. Range   D. Off Cycle

92. D   One thousandth of a millimeter.
A. Accelerate   B. Joule   C. PSC Motor   D. Micron

93. **B** Substance with ability to take up, or absorb another substance.
A. Partial Pressure B. Absorbent C. Absolute Zero Temperature D. Very high pressure

94. **B** Converts high pressure liquid to low pressure vapor
A. Absorber B. Expansion device C. Junction Box D. Orifice Plate

95. **C** A pointed or sharp edged solid substance inserted in flooded type evaporators to improve evaporation (boiling) of refrigerant in coil.
A. Head Pressure B. Refrigeration C. Ebulator D. Absorbent

96. **D** Any device which contains a refrigerant and which is used for household or commercial purposes, including any air conditioner, refrigerator, chiller, or freezer.
A. Evaporator B. Adiabatic Compression C. Calorimeter D. Appliance

97. **B** The process of cooling or chilling.
A. Receiver Heating Element B. Refrigeration C. Decibel D. Filter

98. **A** A substance produces a refrigerating or cooling effect while expanding or vaporizing.
A. Refrigerant B. Farad C. Pressure D. Calcium Sulfate

99. **B** A standard unit of measure for electrical resistance.
A. Recycle B. OHM C. Refrigerant D. Test Light

100. **B** Device which releases the contents of a container above normal pressures, and before rupture pressures are reached.
A. Filter B. Safety Plug C. Kelvin D. Dehydration Evacuation

B. From the words provided for each clue, provide the letter of the word which best matches the clue.

1. **C** The parts of an appliance that are normally connected to each other and are designed to contain refrigerant.
A. Rupture disc B. Absolute Humidity C. Refrigerant circuit D. Dew Point

2. **D** A refrigerant has a boiling point above 10C or 50F at atmospheric pressure.
A. Vacuum Gauge B. Disposable cylinders C. Joule D. Low pressure

3. **B** A temperature control device. Typically mounted in conditioned space.
A. Halide Refrigerants B. Thermostat C. Junction Box D. Piston Displacement

4. **A** Control used to open or close electrical circuits as temperature or pressure limits are reached.
A. Limit Control B. Rupture disc C. Kelvin D. Boyles Law

5. **B** Typically, a multi ported valve used by service technicians to isolate remote system components, as well as check pressures and charge refrigerating units.
A. ACR Tubing B. Service Valve C. Montreal Protocol D. Dew Point

6. **B** A substance formed by a union of two or more elements
A. Absolute Pressure B. Compound C. Evaporator D. Decibel

7. **A** Valve actuated by magnetic action by means of an electrically energized coil.
A. Solenoid Valve B. Range C. Dew Point D. Vacuum Control System

8. **C** A device equipped with gauges and manual valves, used by serviceman to service refrigerating systems.
A. Gas B. Therm C. Service Manifold D. Eddy Currents

9. **D** A pressure imposed upon a fluid is transmitted equally in all directions.
A. Absorber B. Induction Motor C. Disposable cylinders D. Pascals Law

10. __D__ Device or instrument such as a halide torch, an electronic sniffer; or soap solution used to detect leaks.
A. Vacuum Pump   B. Calorimeter   C. Storage cylinders   D. Leak Detector

11. __B__ Converts high pressure liquid to low pressure vapor
A. Adsorption   B. Expansion device   C. Appliance   D. Pinch off Tool

12. __C__ The temperature at which the non-azeotropic blend first begins to condense.
A. Density   B. Farad   C. Dew Point   D. Absorbent

13. __B__ A chemical used in fire extinguishing.
A. Atmosphere   B. Halon   C. ACR Tubing   D. Latent Heat

14. __A__ Invisible energy caused by the motion of molecules within any substance or matter.
A. Heat   B. Junction Box   C. Velocity Head   D. Evaporator Coil

15. __C__ To determine; position indicators as required to obtain accurate measurements.
A. Temperature Glide   B. Pascals Law   C. Calibrate   D. Junction Box

16. __A__ To remove refrigerant in any condition from an appliance and store it in an external container without necessarily testing or processing it in any way.
A. Recover   B. Joule   C. Calibrate   D. Storage cylinders

17. __A__ Part of stator of motor which concentrates magnetic field of field winding.
A. Field Pole   B. Pressure   C. Refrigeration   D. Gas

18. __A__ A passive throttling device, comprised of a small opening, located upstream of the evaporator.
A. Orifice Plate   B. Capacitance   C. Evaporator   D. Isomer

19. __B__ An independent refrigeration system that separates the non-condensables from the refrigerant and re-condenses and collects any refrigerant in the exhaust vent stream.
A. Saddle Valve   B. Purge unit   C. Distillation   D. Heat Exchanger

20. __A__ Instrument used to measure pressures below atmospheric pressure.
A. Vacuum Gauge   B. Damper   C. Pinch off Tool   D. Fractionation

21. __C__ High Pressure
A. Mixture   B. Orifice Plate   C. Red   D. Temperature

22. __D__ Unit of electrical power, equal to 1000 watts.
A. Econimizer   B. Therm   C. Evaporator Coil   D. Kilometer

23. __B__ The piping used to connect the outdoor unit to the indoor unit.
A. Saddle Valve   B. Line Set   C. Field Pole   D. Absorbent

24. __A__ The process of extracting any air, non-condensable gases, or water from the system.
A. Evacuation   B. Montreal Protocol   C. Absorbent   D. Recycle

25. __D__ Substance used to counteract acids, in refrigeration system.
A. Dehydrate   B. Vacuum   C. Absorption Chiller   D. Neutralizer

26. __A__ Unit of measure referring to the flow of electrons within a circuit.
A. Ampere   B. Fan   C. Eddy Currents   D. Chlorine

27. __D__ The process in which a gas flows through a small hole in a container.
A. Temperature Glide   B. Micron   C. Absolute Zero Temperature   D. Effusion

28. __D__ Heat energy absorbed in process of changing form of substance without change in temperature or pressure.
A. Neutralizer   B. Ohms Law   C. Refrigeration   D. Latent Heat

29. C Compressing refrigerant gas without removing or adding heat.
A. Small appliance   B. Heat   C. Adiabatic Compression   D. Insulation

30. A Creates pressure drop to allow liquid refrigerant to boil and absorb latent heat.
A. Metering Device   B. Boyles Law   C. De Minimus   D. Low pressure

31. A An AC motor which operates on principle of rotating magnetic field. Rotor has no electrical connection, but receives electrical energy by transformer action from field windings.
A. Induction Motor   B. Air   C. Zeotropic   D. Ohmmeter

32. D Any material or substance which has the ability to retard the flow or transfer of heat.
A. Ohms Law   B. Saddle Valve   C. OHM   D. Insulation

33. A Light provided with test leads, used to test or probe electrical circuits to determine if they are alive.
A. Test Light   B. Halide Torch   C. Adsorbent   D. Refrigerant

34. A protects equipment or system from over pressurization or damaging vacuum conditions.
A. Rupture disc   B. Accumulator   C. Absorber   D. Latent Heat

35. A A law stating that the volume of a Gas at a given temperature varies inversely with the applied pressure.
A. Boyles Law   B. Actuator   C. Metering Device   D. Psychrometer

36. D Accumulates any low pressure liquid from the evaporator so it can vaporize before entering the compressor
A. Activated Carbon   B. OHM   C. Latent Heat   D. Accumulator

37. C A mixture of at least two different liquids.
A. Latent Heat   B. Head Pressure   C. Azeotroph   D. Actuator

38. B Side by side and having the same distance continuously between them.
A. Latent Heat   B. Parallel   C. Halon   D. Induction Motor

39. C Condition in which refrigerant and
A. Accelerate   B. Calibrate   C. Acid Condition   D. Activated Alumina

40. C Electrical resistance mounted in or around liquid receiver, used to maintain head pressures when ambient temperature is at freezing or below freezing.
A. Thermostat   B. Kelvin   C. Receiver Heating Element   D. Adiabatic Compression

41. A Round or rectangular pipes or controlled paths acting as conduit for return, mixed, makeup, supply or exhaust air.
A. Ductwork   B. Bubble Point   C. Density   D. Refrigerant

42. B High-efficiency design motor used on virtually all of today's HVAC & R equipment requiring motors.
A. Isolate   B. PSC Motor   C. Limit Control   D. Hydrostatic

43. B States that the volume occupied by a gas at a constant Pressure is directly proportional to the absolute temperature.
A. Compound   B. Charles Law   C. Halide Refrigerants   D. Off Cycle

44. A Gauge pressure plus atmospheric pressure (14.7 lbs. per sq. in.).
A. Absolute Pressure   B. Actuator   C. Compressor   D. High pressure

45. D One thousandth of a millimeter.
A. Joule   B. Fan   C. Manometer   D. Micron

46. D The process of collecting used refrigerant.
A. Recover   B. De Minimus   C. Service Valve   D. Recovery

47. D The SI base unit of temperature; a unit on an absolute temperature scale.
A. Opening   B. Super Heat   C. Reclaim   D. Kelvin

48. __C__ A substance produces a refrigerating or cooling effect while expanding or vaporizing.
A. British Thermal Unit   B. Watt   C. Refrigerant   D. Recover

49. __C__ That time period of a refrigeration cycle when the system is not operating.
A. Ampere   B. Storage cylinders   C. Off Cycle   D. Small appliance

50. __D__ Either a sling type, or electronic. Instrument used to determine wet bulb temperatures and relative humidity.
A. Micron   B. Temperature Glide   C. Saturation Temperature   D. Psychrometer

51. __D__ Tubing used in refrigeration which has ends to keep tubing clean and dry.
A. Humidity   B. Blue   C. Halon   D. ACR Tubing

52. __B__ The form of matter that is an easily compressible fluid
A. Temperature   B. Gas   C. Accumulator   D. Volt

53. __A__ Substance with ability to take up, or absorb another substance.
A. Absorbent   B. Service Manifold   C. Humidity   D. Vacuum

54. __D__ Device used to measure quantities of heat or determine specific heats.
A. Thermostat   B. Accelerate   C. Vacuum   D. Calorimeter

55. __C__ Receives high pressure liquid from the condenser
A. Red   B. Therm   C. Receiver   D. Leak Detector

56. __D__ The process of cooling or chilling.
A. Absolute Pressure   B. Disposable cylinders   C. Volt   D. Refrigeration

57. __D__ To remove water from a system.
A. Field Pole   B. Ultraviolet Radiation   C. Eddy Currents   D. Dehydrate

58. __B__ The moving of heat from an undesirable location, to that of a location where its presence is less undesirable.
A. Piston Displacement   B. Refrigeration   C. Volt   D. Montreal Protocol

59. __B__ Pressure in low side of refrigerating system; also called suction pressure or low side pressure.
A. Chlorine   B. Back Pressure   C. Reusable cylinders   D. Service Manifold

60. __D__ Evaporates low pressure vapor from the expansion device
A. Vapor   B. Safety Plug   C. Farad   D. Evaporator

61. __C__ A radial or axial flow device used for moving or producing artificial currents of air.
A. Metering Device   B. Acid Condition   C. Fan   D. Humidity

62. __D__ A compound containing only the elements hydrogen and carbon.
A. Safety Motor Control   B. Heat Exchanger   C. Adsorption   D. Hydrocarbon

63. __D__ Single use cylinders. Empty cylinders should have the pressure reduced to zero and the cylinder rendered unusable.
A. Chlorine   B. Activated Alumina   C. Head Pressure   D. Disposable cylinders

64. __B__ Induced currents flowing in a core.
A. Accumulator   B. Eddy Currents   C. Vacuum Gauge   D. Ohmmeter

65. __B__ Each refrigerant in the blend keeps its own temperature and pressure characteristics.
A. Vacuum   B. Zeotropic   C. Damper   D. Fan

66. __C__ A form of testing for high pressure cylinders.
A. Recovery   B. Refrigeration   C. Hydrostatic   D. Isomer

67. B Any products that are fully manufactured, charged, and hermetically sealed in a factory with five pounds or less of refrigerant
A. Metering Device   B. Small appliance   C. Center port   D. Effusion

68. C Reduction in pressure below atmospheric pressure.
A. Adsorbent   B. Compressor   C. Vacuum   D. Back Seating

69. D Mathematical relationships between voltage, current and resistance in an electric circuit, discovered by George Simon Ohm.
A. Leak Rate   B. Chlorine   C. Diffusion   D. Ohms Law

70. C The action of purifying a liquid by a process of heating and cooling.
A. De Minimus   B. Vapor   C. Distillation   D. Absolute Humidity

71. C The total amount of moisture in air.
A. Air   B. Leak Detector   C. Humidity   D. Compound

72. C To extract refrigerant from an appliance and clean refrigerant for reuse without meeting all of the requirements for reclamation.
A. Kelvin   B. Technician   C. Recycle   D. Vacuum

73. A Any maintenance or repair on an appliance that would release refrigerant from the appliance to the atmosphere.
A. Opening   B. Orifice Plate   C. Actuator   D. Refrigerant

74. A Group of electrical terminals housed in protective box or container.
A. Junction Box   B. Micron   C. Ebulator   D. Heat

75. D Instrument to measuring pressure of gases and vapors.
A. Opening   B. Recycle   C. Off Cycle   D. Manometer

76. B The difference between the Dew Point and the Bubble Point.
A. Storage cylinders   B. Temperature Glide   C. Adiabatic Compression   D. Absorber

77. B Requires the assistance of components such as the appliance or unit's compressor to remove the refrigerant from the appliance.
A. Vacuum Gauge   B. Passive recovery   C. Flame Test   D. Activated Carbon

78. C Unit of electrical capacity; capacity of a condenser which, when charged with one coulomb of electricity, gives difference of potential of one volt.
A. Montreal Protocol   B. Boyles Law   C. Farad   D. Psychrometer

79. D Any person who performs maintenance, service, or repair that could reasonably be expected to release class I or class II substances into the atmosphere.
A. Absorbent   B. Recycle   C. Absolute Humidity   D. Technician

80. C The process whereby a gas spreads out through another gas to occupy the space with uniform partial Pressure.
A. Micron   B. Orifice Plate   C. Diffusion   D. Chlorine

81. B Latin for the least amount of Refrigerant you can release into the atmosphere.
A. Volt   B. De Minimus   C. Activated Alumina   D. Compound gauge

82. C The force exerted per unit area of surface.
A. Halide Torch   B. Ohms Law   C. Pressure   D. Junction Box

83. D Tool which is principally a torch and when an air refrigerant mixture is fed to flame, this flame will change color in presence of heated copper.
A. Montreal Protocol   B. Ozone layer   C. Mixture   D. Flame Test

84. D A standard unit of measure for electrical resistance.
A. Red   B. Micron   C. Range   D. OHM

85. __A__ The temperature at which the non-azeotropic blend first begins to evaporate.
   A. Bubble Point   B. Absolute Pressure   C. Ultraviolet Radiation   D. Volt

86. __B__ Special high efficiency device (pump) used create deep vacuum within an AC
   A. Service Valve   B. Vacuum Pump   C. Absolute Humidity   D. Fan

87. __D__ Unit of electrical power.
   A. Montreal Protocol   B. Safety Motor Control   C. Fractionation   D. Watt

88. __D__ Need to evacuate system to eliminate air and moisture at the end of service.
   A. Therm   B. Hydrostatic   C. Orifice Plate   D. Dehydration Evacuation

89. __D__ Pressure of fluid expressed in terms of height of column of the fluid, such as water or mercury.
   A. Range   B. Orifice Plate   C. Absorbent   D. Static Head

90. __C__ A tool that measures pressure readings at different points in the refrigeration system.
   A. Back Pressure   B. Low pressure   C. Gauge manifold   D. Back Seating

91. __A__ Vapor phase or state of a substance.
   A. Gas   B. Small appliance   C. Hydrostatic   D. Effusion

92. __D__ Device for removing small particles from a fluid.
   A. Halide Torch   B. Evaporator   C. Purge unit   D. Filter

93. __A__ Pressure or temperature settings of a control; change within limits.
   A. Range   B. Fractionation   C. Thermostat   D. Miscible

94. __C__ Converting recycled refrigerant into a product to be reused.
   A. Metering Device   B. Density   C. Reclaim   D. Diffusion

95. __D__ The Gaseous state of any kind of matter that normally exists as a liquid or solid.
   A. Absolute Temperature   B. Safety Control   C. Pinch off Tool   D. Vapor

96. __D__ Measures low pressure and vacuum.
   A. Absorbent   B. Disposable cylinders   C. Vacuum Control System   D. Compound gauge

97. __C__ A blend of two or more components that do not a have fixed proportion to one another.
   A. Junction Box   B. Damper   C. Mixture   D. Diffusion

98. __D__ Any device which contains a refrigerant and which is used for household or commercial purposes, including any air
   conditioner, refrigerator, chiller, or freezer.
   A. Center port   B. Limit Control   C. Vacuum Pump   D. Appliance

99. __B__ Amount of moisture in the air, indicated in grains per cubic foot.
   A. Bubble Point   B. Absolute Humidity   C. Recover   D. Storage cylinders

100. __C__ The temperature where a refrigerant exists in both liquid and vapor form relative to its measured pressure.
   A. Wet Bulb   B. Absorption Chiller   C. Saturation Temperature   D. Pressure

Matching

A. Provide the word that best matches each clue.

1. _____ Creates pressure drop to allow liquid refrigerant to boil and absorb latent heat.

2. _____ Any products that are fully manufactured, charged, and hermetically sealed in a factory with five pounds or less of refrigerant

3. _____ Pressure in low side of refrigerating system; also called suction pressure or low side pressure.

4. _____ Quantity of heat equivalent to 100,000 Btu.

5. _____ Device used to electrically shut down a refrigerating unit when unsafe pressures and

6. _____ The SI base unit of temperature; a unit on an absolute temperature scale.

7. _____ A mixture of at least two different liquids.

8. _____ Instrument used to measure pressures below atmospheric pressure.

9. _____ A substance formed by a union of two or more elements

10. _____ Device used to press walls of a tubing together until fluid flow ceases.

11. _____ Substance which has property to hold molecules of fluids without causing a chemical or physical change.

12. _____ A blend of two or more components that do not a have fixed proportion to one another.

13. _____ Device which releases the contents of a container above normal pressures, and before rupture pressures are reached.

14. _____ Control used to open or close electrical circuits as temperature or pressure limits are reached.

15. _____ The temperature at which the non-azeotropic blend first begins to condense.

16. _____ Low pressure

17. _____ Gas used for leak detection.

18. _____ In flowing fluid, height of fluid equivalent to its velocity pressure.

19. _____ Any maintenance or repair on an appliance that would release refrigerant from the appliance to the atmosphere.

20. _____ cause to be or remain alone or apart from others.

21. _____ Light provided with test leads, used to test or probe electrical circuits to determine if they are alive.

22. _____ The total amount of moisture in air.

23. _____ Unit of electrical power, equal to 1000 watts.

24. _____ Invisible, odorless, and tasteless mixture of gases which form earth's atmosphere.

25. _____ Measures low pressure and vacuum.

A. Adsorbent   B. Isolate   C. Velocity Head   D. Air
E. Compound gauge   F. Opening   G. Kilometer   H. Back Pressure
I. Test Light   J. Compound   K. Blue   L. Pinch off Tool
M. Azeotroph   N. Limit Control   O. Therm   P. Nitrogen
Q. Dew Point   R. Safety Plug   S. Vacuum Gauge   T. Humidity
U. Safety Control   V. Small appliance   W. Kelvin   X. Mixture
Y. Metering Device

B. Provide the word that best matches each clue.

1. _____ Where heat is absorbed by warm air passing across. Liquid refrigerant boils as it is metered into coil, and changes from liquid to vapor.

2. _____ In flowing fluid, height of fluid equivalent to its velocity pressure.

3. _____ Pressure or temperature settings of a control; change within limits.

4. _____ A compound containing only the elements hydrogen and carbon.

5. _____ A combination shut-off and service value typically used on the inlet and outlet of a compressor.

6. _____ Specially processed carbon used as a filter drier; commonly used to clean air.

7. _____ The action of purifying a liquid by a process of heating and cooling.

8. _____ Temperature measured from absolute zero.

9. _____ Device used to press walls of a tubing together until fluid flow ceases.

10. _____ Family of refrigerants containing halogen chemicals.

11. _____ The fluid used for heat transfer in a refrigeration system, which absorbs heat during evaporation at low temperature and pressure, and releases heat during condensation.

12. _____ Type of torch used to detect halogen refrigerant leaks.

13. _____ Any material or substance which has the ability to retard the flow or transfer of heat.

14. _____ A substance formed by a union of two or more elements

15. _____ Valve actuated by magnetic action by means of an electrically energized coil.

16. _____ A unit of Pressure equal to exactly 760 mmHg

17. _____ A device for the transfer of heat energy from the source to the conveying medium, with the latter often being air or water.

18. _____ Quantity of heat equivalent to 100,000 Btu.

19. _____ Tubing used in refrigeration which has ends to keep tubing clean and dry.

20. _____ A chemical used in fire extinguishing.

21. _____ A passive throttling device, comprised of a small opening, located upstream of the evaporator.

22. _____ To determine; position indicators as required to obtain accurate measurements.

23. _____ The atom found in CFC and HCFC refrigerants that destroys ozone in the stratosphere.

24. _____ Part of stator of motor which concentrates magnetic field of field winding.

25. _____ The force exerted per unit area of surface.

A. Velocity Head
B. Heat Exchanger
C. Chlorine
D. Activated Carbon
E. Therm
F. Evaporator Coil
G. Halide Refrigerants
H. Orifice Plate
I. Hydrocarbon
J. Atmosphere
K. Calibrate
L. Absolute Temperature
M. Solenoid Valve
N. Refrigerant
O. Halide Torch
P. Compound
Q. Insulation
R. Halon
S. Distillation
T. Pinch off Tool
U. ACR Tubing
V. King Valve
W. Field Pole
X. Pressure
Y. Range

C. Provide the word that best matches each clue.

1. _____ Tubing used in refrigeration which has ends to keep tubing clean and dry.

2. _____ A refrigerant has a boiling point between minus 50C and 10C degrees at atmospheric pressure.

3. _____ The process of extracting any air, non-condensable gases, or water from the system.

4. _____ Change in temperature of a gas on expansion through a porous plug from a high pressure to a lower pressure.

5. _____ To determine; position indicators as required to obtain accurate measurements.

6. _____ Low pressure

7. _____ The process of collecting used refrigerant.

8. _____ Where heat is absorbed by warm air passing across. Liquid refrigerant boils as it is metered into coil, and changes from liquid to vapor.

9. _____ Gray cylinder with a yellow top; used for recovery or transporting refrigerant.

10. _____ A compound containing only the elements hydrogen and carbon.

11. _____ Type of torch used to detect halogen refrigerant leaks.

12. _____ Pressure which exists in condensing side of refrigerating system.

13. _____ The temperature where a refrigerant exists in both liquid and vapor form relative to its measured pressure.

14. _____ Electrical "pressure" applied to a circuit.

15. _____ Tool which is principally a torch and when an air refrigerant mixture is fed to flame, this flame will change color in presence of heated copper.

16. _____ Invisible energy caused by the motion of molecules within any substance or matter.

17. _____ Side by side and having the same distance continuously between them.

18. _____ A radial or axial flow device used for moving or producing artificial currents of air.

19. _____ That time period of a refrigeration cycle when the system is not operating.

20. _____ Device used in measurement of relative humidity. Evaporation of moisture lowers temperature of wet bulb compared to dry bulb temperature in same area.

21. _____ The difference between the Dew Point and the Bubble Point.

22. _____ The fluid used for heat transfer in a refrigeration system, which absorbs heat during evaporation at low temperature and pressure, and releases heat during condensation.

23. _____ A combination shut-off and service value typically used on the inlet and outlet of a compressor.

24. _____ Device used to press walls of a tubing together until fluid flow ceases.

25. _____ Process whereas additional sensible heat (as opposed to latent heat) is removed from condensed refrigerant liquid prior to the metering device.

A. Joule   B. Head Pressure   C. King Valve
D. Refrigerant   E. Recovery   F. Fan
G. High pressure   H. Evacuation   I. Halide Torch
J. Parallel   K. Flame Test   L. Sub Cooling
M. Evaporator Coil   N. Pinch off Tool   O. Saturation Temperature
P. Calibrate   Q. Temperature Glide   R. Off Cycle
S. Wet Bulb   T. Heat   U. ACR Tubing
V. Hydrocarbon   W. Volt   X. Reusable cylinders
Y. Blue

D. Provide the word that best matches each clue.

1. _____ The process of collecting used refrigerant.

2. _____ A refrigerant has a boiling point below minus 50C or minus 58F at atmospheric pressure.

3. _____ Electrical "pressure" applied to a circuit.

4. _____ Gray cylinder with a yellow top; used for recovery or transporting refrigerant.

5. _____ Any person who performs maintenance, service, or repair that could reasonably be expected to release class I or class II substances into the atmosphere.

6. _____ Need to evacuate system to eliminate air and moisture at the end of service.

7. _____ Breaks down the CFCs and frees the chlorine ion at stratosphere.

8. _____ Any maintenance or repair on an appliance that would release refrigerant from the appliance to the atmosphere.

9. _____ Treaty among nations designed to protect the stratospheric ozone layer.

10. _____ Refrigerator which creates low temperatures by using the cooling effect formed when a refrigerant is absorbed by chemical substance.

11. _____ Volume displaced by piston as it travels length of stroke.

12. _____ Device which releases the contents of a container above normal pressures, and before rupture pressures are reached.

13. _____ Family of refrigerants containing halogen chemicals.

14. _____ Any material or substance which has the ability to retard the flow or transfer of heat.

15. _____ An independent refrigeration system that separates the non-condensables from the refrigerant and re-condenses and collects any refrigerant in the exhaust vent stream.

16. _____ A mechanism that removes flash gas from the evaporator.

17. _____ Evaporates low pressure vapor from the expansion device

18. _____ The form of matter that is an easily compressible fluid

19. _____ A pointed or sharp edged solid substance inserted in flooded type evaporators to improve evaporation (boiling) of refrigerant in coil.

20. _____ Device used to electrically shut down a refrigerating unit when unsafe pressures and

21. _____ Invisible energy caused by the motion of molecules within any substance or matter.

22. _____ Where heat is absorbed by warm air passing across. Liquid refrigerant boils as it is metered into coil, and changes from liquid to vapor.

23. _____ Pressure which exists in condensing side of refrigerating system.

24. _____ Unit of measure referring to the flow of electrons within a circuit.

25. _____ Larger cylinders used for storing refrigerant to be transferred to smaller refillable cylinders.

A. Storage cylinders	B. Head Pressure	C. Insulation
D. Evaporator	E. Ebulator	F. Absorption Refrigerator
G. Econimizer	H. Ampere	I. Safety Control
J. Montreal Protocol	K. Purge unit	L. Very high pressure
M. Technician	N. Piston Displacement	O. Dehydration Evacuation
P. Halide Refrigerants	Q. Reusable cylinders	R. Gas
S. Evaporator Coil	T. Safety Plug	U. Volt
V. Ultraviolet Radiation	W. Opening	X. Recovery
Y. Heat		

E. Provide the word that best matches each clue.

1. _____ Converting recycled refrigerant into a product to be reused.

2. _____ Dissipates heat from the refrigerant.

3. _____ A tool that measures pressure readings at different points in the refrigeration system.

4. _____ Specially processed carbon used as a filter drier; commonly used to clean air.

5. _____ Control used to open or close electrical circuits as temperature or pressure limits are reached.

6. _____ Unit of electrical capacity; capacity of a condenser which, when charged with one coulomb of electricity, gives difference of potential of one volt.

7. _____ Change in temperature of a gas on expansion through a porous plug from a high pressure to a lower pressure.

8. _____ The temperature where a refrigerant exists in both liquid and vapor form relative to its measured pressure.

9. _____ Special high efficiency device (pump) used create deep vacuum within an AC

10. _____ Quantity of heat equivalent to 100,000 Btu.

11. _____ Converts high pressure liquid to low pressure vapor

12. _____ A mechanism that removes flash gas from the evaporator.

13. _____ Gas phase

14. _____ Typically, a multi ported valve used by service technicians to isolate remote system components, as well as check pressures and charge refrigerating units.

15. _____ Instrument to measuring pressure of gases and vapors.

16. _____ A temperature scale in which the lowest temperature that can be attained theoretically is zero

17. _____ Valve actuated by magnetic action by means of an electrically energized coil.

18. _____ The piping used to connect the outdoor unit to the indoor unit.

19. _____ Undesirable component in many refrigeration lubricants, which may separate out of solution if cooled sufficiently.

20. _____ Electrical "pressure" applied to a circuit.

21. _____ The atom found in CFC and HCFC refrigerants that destroys ozone in the stratosphere.

22. _____ Substance which has property to hold molecules of fluids without causing a chemical or physical change.

23. _____ Degree of hotness or coldness as measured by a thermometer

24. _____ Temperature measured from absolute zero.

25. _____ Property of non-conductor that permits storage of electrical energy in an electrostatic field.

A. Limit Control	B. Wax	C. Manometer
D. Therm	E. Absolute Temperature	F. Vapor
G. Service Valve	H. Vacuum Pump	I. Condenser Coil
J. Reclaim	K. Joule	L. Saturation Temperature
M. Absolute Temperature	N. Expansion device	O. Activated Carbon
P. Econimizer	Q. Solenoid Valve	R. Line Set
S. Adsorbent	T. Capacitance	U. Farad
V. Volt	W. Temperature	X. Gauge manifold
Y. Chlorine		

F. Provide the word that best matches each clue.

1. _____ Vapor phase or state of a substance.

2. _____ Degree of hotness or coldness as measured by a thermometer

3. _____ A radial or axial flow device used for moving or producing artificial currents of air.

4. _____ Property of non-conductor that permits storage of electrical energy in an electrostatic field.

5. _____ Tool which is principally a torch and when an air refrigerant mixture is fed to flame, this flame will change color in presence of heated copper.

6. _____ An instrument for measuring resistance in ohms.

7. _____ A pointed or sharp edged solid substance inserted in flooded type evaporators to improve evaporation (boiling) of refrigerant in coil.

8. _____ The form of matter that is an easily compressible fluid

9. _____ The temperature rise within an evaporator or suction line assembly from the evaporator's saturation temperature.

10. _____ Device for removing small particles from a fluid.

11. _____ Side by side and having the same distance continuously between them.

12. _____ A unit of measurement used for determining cooling capacity. One ton is the equivalent of 12,000 BTUs per hour.

13. _____ A refrigerant has a boiling point between minus 50C and 10C degrees at atmospheric pressure.

14. _____ Round or rectangular pipes or controlled paths acting as conduit for return, mixed, makeup, supply or exhaust air.

15. _____ A separation process in which a certain quantity of a mixture is divided during a phase transition

16. _____ protects equipment or system from over pressurization or damaging vacuum conditions.

17. _____ A temperature control device. Typically mounted in conditioned space.

18. _____ Pressure of fluid expressed in terms of height of column of the fluid, such as water or mercury.

19. _____ Device used to electrically shut down a refrigerating unit when unsafe pressures and

20. _____ A mechanism that removes flash gas from the evaporator.

21. _____ Electrical resistance mounted in or around liquid receiver, used to maintain head pressures when ambient temperature is at freezing or below freezing.

22. _____ Unit of electrical power.

23. _____ The atom found in CFC and HCFC refrigerants that destroys ozone in the stratosphere.

24. _____ Gray cylinder with a yellow top; used for recovery or transporting refrigerant.

25. _____ High-efficiency design motor used on virtually all of today's HVAC & R equipment requiring motors.

A. Reusable cylinders	B. Econimizer	C. Gas
D. Temperature	E. Chlorine	F. Safety Control
G. Watt	H. Ebulator	I. Ductwork
J. Flame Test	K. Fractionation	L. Capacitance
M. Ohmmeter	N. Thermostat	O. Parallel
P. Receiver Heating Element	Q. Static Head	R. Gas
S. PSC Motor	T. TON	U. Super Heat
V. Rupture disc	W. High pressure	X. Fan
Y. Filter		

G. Provide the word that best matches each clue.

1. _____ A radial or axial flow device used for moving or producing artificial currents of air.

2. _____ An AC motor which operates on principle of rotating magnetic field. Rotor has no electrical connection, but receives electrical energy by transformer action from field windings.

3. _____ In flowing fluid, height of fluid equivalent to its velocity pressure.

4. _____ In some air conditioning systems, vacuum is used to operate dampers and controls in system.

5. _____ Gauge pressure plus atmospheric pressure (14.7 lbs. per sq. in.).

6. _____ Type of torch used to detect halogen refrigerant leaks.

7. _____ Protective shield for Earth from the sun's harmful ultraviolet (UV) rays in the stratosphere layer that extends about 6 to 30 miles above earth.

8. _____ The rate at which an appliance is losing refrigerant.

9. _____ The total amount of moisture in air.

10. _____ Instrument used to measure pressures below atmospheric pressure.

11. _____ Electrical device used to open circuit if the temperature, pressure, and

12. _____ Amount of moisture in the air, indicated in grains per cubic foot.

13. _____ Induced currents flowing in a core.

14. _____ Gas phase

15. _____ Forming a homogeneous mixture of liquids when added together.

16. _____ Pressure or temperature settings of a control; change within limits.

17. _____ That time period of a refrigeration cycle when the system is not operating.

18. _____ Device used to electrically shut down a refrigerating unit when unsafe pressures and

19. _____ A unit of Pressure equal to exactly 760 mmHg

20. _____ High Pressure

21. _____ Gas used for leak detection.

22. _____ Close fitting part which moves up and down in a cylinder.

23. _____ The temperature at which the non-azeotropic blend first begins to evaporate.

24. _____ The form of matter that is an easily compressible fluid

25. _____ Pressure which exists in condensing side of refrigerating system.

A. Piston	B. Head Pressure	C. Leak Rate
D. Humidity	E. Safety Motor Control	F. Velocity Head
G. Red	H. Vacuum Control System	I. Bubble Point
J. Vapor	K. Ozone layer	L. Gas
M. Vacuum Gauge	N. Range	O. Safety Control
P. Nitrogen	Q. Eddy Currents	R. Miscible
S. Induction Motor	T. Absolute Humidity	U. Atmosphere
V. Halide Torch	W. Fan	X. Absolute Pressure
Y. Off Cycle		

H. Provide the word that best matches each clue.

1. _____ An independent refrigeration system that separates the non-condensables from the refrigerant and re-condenses and collects any refrigerant in the exhaust vent stream.

2. _____ Device used in measurement of relative humidity. Evaporation of moisture lowers temperature of wet bulb compared to dry bulb temperature in same area.

3. _____ A device equipped with gauges and manual valves, used by serviceman to service refrigerating systems.

4. _____ Instrument used to measure pressures below atmospheric pressure.

5. _____ The SI base unit of temperature; a unit on an absolute temperature scale.

6. _____ Side by side and having the same distance continuously between them.

7. _____ The mass per unit volume of a substance or solution.

8. _____ A combination shut-off and service value typically used on the inlet and outlet of a compressor.

9. _____ The total amount of moisture in air.

10. _____ Pressure in low side of refrigerating system; also called suction pressure or low side pressure.

11. _____ A device for the transfer of heat energy from the source to the conveying medium, with the latter often being air or water.

12. _____ Induced currents flowing in a core.

13. _____ The atom found in CFC and HCFC refrigerants that destroys ozone in the stratosphere.

14. _____ Tubing used in refrigeration which has ends to keep tubing clean and dry.

15. _____ The temperature at which the non-azeotropic blend first begins to condense.

16. _____ Temperature measured from absolute zero.

17. _____ Process whereas additional sensible heat (as opposed to latent heat) is removed from condensed refrigerant liquid prior to the metering device.

18. _____ Invisible energy caused by the motion of molecules within any substance or matter.

19. _____ The form of matter that is an easily compressible fluid

20. _____ Latin for the least amount of Refrigerant you can release into the atmosphere.

21. _____ To extract refrigerant from an appliance and clean refrigerant for reuse without meeting all of the requirements for reclamation.

22. _____ Condenses high pressure gas from the compressor to high pressure liquid.

23. _____ Device used to measure quantities of heat or determine specific heats.

24. _____ Device for removing small particles from a fluid.

25. _____ protects equipment or system from over pressurization or damaging vacuum conditions.

A. Rupture disc	B. Filter	C. Condenser
D. Gas	E. Eddy Currents	F. Density
G. Recycle	H. Calorimeter	I. Heat Exchanger
J. ACR Tubing	K. Service Manifold	L. De Minimus
M. Dew Point	N. Parallel	O. Sub Cooling
P. Purge unit	Q. King Valve	R. Absolute Temperature
S. Humidity	T. Vacuum Gauge	U. Chlorine
V. Kelvin	W. Back Pressure	X. Heat
Y. Wet Bulb		

A. Provide the word that best matches each clue.

1. METERING DEVICE — Creates pressure drop to allow liquid refrigerant to boil and absorb latent heat.

2. SMALL APPLIANCE — Any products that are fully manufactured, charged, and hermetically sealed in a factory with five pounds or less of refrigerant

3. BACK PRESSURE — Pressure in low side of refrigerating system; also called suction pressure or low side pressure.

4. THERM — Quantity of heat equivalent to 100,000 Btu.

5. SAFETY CONTROL — Device used to electrically shut down a refrigerating unit when unsafe pressures and

6. KELVIN — The SI base unit of temperature; a unit on an absolute temperature scale.

7. AZEOTROPH — A mixture of at least two different liquids.

8. VACUUM GAUGE — Instrument used to measure pressures below atmospheric pressure.

9. COMPOUND — A substance formed by a union of two or more elements

10. PINCH OFF TOOL — Device used to press walls of a tubing together until fluid flow ceases.

11. ADSORBENT — Substance which has property to hold molecules of fluids without causing a chemical or physical change.

12. MIXTURE — A blend of two or more components that do not a have fixed proportion to one another.

13. SAFETY PLUG — Device which releases the contents of a container above normal pressures, and before rupture pressures are reached.

14. LIMIT CONTROL — Control used to open or close electrical circuits as temperature or pressure limits are reached.

15. DEW POINT — The temperature at which the non-azeotropic blend first begins to condense.

16. BLUE — Low pressure

17. NITROGEN — Gas used for leak detection.

18. VELOCITY HEAD — In flowing fluid, height of fluid equivalent to its velocity pressure.

19. OPENING — Any maintenance or repair on an appliance that would release refrigerant from the appliance to the atmosphere.

20. ISOLATE — cause to be or remain alone or apart from others.

21. TEST LIGHT — Light provided with test leads, used to test or probe electrical circuits to determine if they are alive.

22. HUMIDITY — The total amount of moisture in air.

23. KILOMETER — Unit of electrical power, equal to 1000 watts.

24. AIR — Invisible, odorless, and tasteless mixture of gases which form earth's atmosphere.

25. COMPOUND GAUGE — Measures low pressure and vacuum.

A. Adsorbent
B. Isolate
C. Velocity Head
D. Air
E. Compound gauge
F. Opening
G. Kilometer
H. Back Pressure
I. Test Light
J. Compound
K. Blue
L. Pinch off Tool
M. Azeotroph
N. Limit Control
O. Therm
P. Nitrogen
Q. Dew Point
R. Safety Plug
S. Vacuum Gauge
T. Humidity
U. Safety Control
V. Small appliance
W. Kelvin
X. Mixture
Y. Metering Device

B. Provide the word that best matches each clue.

1. EVAPORATOR COIL — Where heat is absorbed by warm air passing across. Liquid refrigerant boils as it is metered into coil, and changes from liquid to vapor.

2. VELOCITY HEAD — In flowing fluid, height of fluid equivalent to its velocity pressure.

3. RANGE — Pressure or temperature settings of a control; change within limits.

4. HYDROCARBON — A compound containing only the elements hydrogen and carbon.

5. KING VALVE — A combination shut-off and service value typically used on the inlet and outlet of a compressor.

6. ACTIVATED CARBON — Specially processed carbon used as a filter drier; commonly used to clean air.

7. DISTILLATION — The action of purifying a liquid by a process of heating and cooling.

8. ABSOLUTE TEMPERATURE — Temperature measured from absolute zero.

9. PINCH OFF TOOL — Device used to press walls of a tubing together until fluid flow ceases.

10. HALIDE REFRIGERANTS — Family of refrigerants containing halogen chemicals.

11. REFRIGERANT — The fluid used for heat transfer in a refrigeration system, which absorbs heat during evaporation at low temperature and pressure, and releases heat during condensation.

12. HALIDE TORCH — Type of torch used to detect halogen refrigerant leaks.

13. INSULATION   Any material or substance which has the ability to retard the flow or transfer of heat.

14. COMPOUND   A substance formed by a union of two or more elements

15. SOLENOID VALVE   Valve actuated by magnetic action by means of an electrically energized coil.

16. ATMOSPHERE   A unit of Pressure equal to exactly 760 mmHg

17. HEAT EXCHANGER   A device for the transfer of heat energy from the source to the conveying medium, with the latter often being air or water.

18. THERM   Quantity of heat equivalent to 100,000 Btu.

19. ACR TUBING   Tubing used in refrigeration which has ends to keep tubing clean and dry.

20. HALON   A chemical used in fire extinguishing.

21. ORIFICE PLATE   A passive throttling device, comprised of a small opening, located upstream of the evaporator.

22. CALIBRATE   To determine; position indicators as required to obtain accurate measurements.

23. CHLORINE   The atom found in CFC and HCFC refrigerants that destroys ozone in the stratosphere.

24. FIELD POLE   Part of stator of motor which concentrates magnetic field of field winding.

25. PRESSURE   The force exerted per unit area of surface.

A. Velocity Head
B. Heat Exchanger
C. Chlorine
D. Activated Carbon
E. Therm
F. Evaporator Coil
G. Halide Refrigerants
H. Orifice Plate
I. Hydrocarbon
J. Atmosphere
K. Calibrate
L. Absolute Temperature
M. Solenoid Valve
N. Refrigerant
O. Halide Torch
P. Compound
Q. Insulation
R. Halon
S. Distillation
T. Pinch off Tool
U. ACR Tubing
V. King Valve
W. Field Pole
X. Pressure
Y. Range

C. Provide the word that best matches each clue.

1. ACR TUBING   Tubing used in refrigeration which has ends to keep tubing clean and dry.

2. HIGH PRESSURE   A refrigerant has a boiling point between minus 50C and 10C degrees at atmospheric pressure.

3. EVACUATION   The process of extracting any air, non-condensable gases, or water from the system.

4. JOULE — Change in temperature of a gas on expansion through a porous plug from a high pressure to a lower pressure.

5. CALIBRATE — To determine; position indicators as required to obtain accurate measurements.

6. BLUE — Low pressure

7. RECOVERY — The process of collecting used refrigerant.

8. EVAPORATOR COIL — Where heat is absorbed by warm air passing across. Liquid refrigerant boils as it is metered into coil, and changes from liquid to vapor.

9. REUSABLE CYLINDERS — Gray cylinder with a yellow top; used for recovery or transporting refrigerant.

10. HYDROCARBON — A compound containing only the elements hydrogen and carbon.

11. HALIDE TORCH — Type of torch used to detect halogen refrigerant leaks.

12. HEAD PRESSURE — Pressure which exists in condensing side of refrigerating system.

13. SATURATION TEMPERATURE — The temperature where a refrigerant exists in both liquid and vapor form relative to its measured pressure.

14. VOLT — Electrical "pressure" applied to a circuit.

15. FLAME TEST — Tool which is principally a torch and when an air refrigerant mixture is fed to flame, this flame will change color in presence of heated copper.

16. HEAT — Invisible energy caused by the motion of molecules within any substance or matter.

17. PARALLEL — Side by side and having the same distance continuously between them.

18. FAN — A radial or axial flow device used for moving or producing artificial currents of air.

19. OFF CYCLE — That time period of a refrigeration cycle when the system is not operating.

20. WET BULB — Device used in measurement of relative humidity. Evaporation of moisture lowers temperature of wet bulb compared to dry bulb temperature in same area.

21. TEMPERATURE GLIDE — The difference between the Dew Point and the Bubble Point.

22. REFRIGERANT — The fluid used for heat transfer in a refrigeration system, which absorbs heat during evaporation at low temperature and pressure, and releases heat during condensation.

23. KING VALVE — A combination shut-off and service value typically used on the inlet and outlet of a compressor.

101

24. PINCH OFF TOOL — Device used to press walls of a tubing together until fluid flow ceases.

25. SUB COOLING — Process whereas additional sensible heat (as opposed to latent heat) is removed from condensed refrigerant liquid prior to the metering device.

A. Joule	B. Head Pressure	C. King Valve
D. Refrigerant	E. Recovery	F. Fan
G. High pressure	H. Evacuation	I. Halide Torch
J. Parallel	K. Flame Test	L. Sub Cooling
M. Evaporator Coil	N. Pinch off Tool	O. Saturation Temperature
P. Calibrate	Q. Temperature Glide	R. Off Cycle
S. Wet Bulb	T. Heat	U. ACR Tubing
V. Hydrocarbon	W. Volt	X. Reusable cylinders
Y. Blue		

D. Provide the word that best matches each clue.

1. RECOVERY — The process of collecting used refrigerant.

2. VERY HIGH PRESSURE — A refrigerant has a boiling point below minus 50C or minus 58F at atmospheric pressure.

3. VOLT — Electrical "pressure" applied to a circuit.

4. REUSABLE CYLINDERS — Gray cylinder with a yellow top; used for recovery or transporting refrigerant.

5. TECHNICIAN — Any person who performs maintenance, service, or repair that could reasonably be expected to release class I or class II substances into the atmosphere.

6. DEHYDRATION EVACUATION — Need to evacuate system to eliminate air and moisture at the end of service.

7. ULTRAVIOLET RADIATION — Breaks down the CFCs and frees the chlorine ion at stratosphere.

8. OPENING — Any maintenance or repair on an appliance that would release refrigerant from the appliance to the atmosphere.

9. MONTREAL PROTOCOL — Treaty among nations designed to protect the stratospheric ozone layer.

10. ABSORPTION REFRIGERATOR — Refrigerator which creates low temperatures by using the cooling effect formed when a refrigerant is absorbed by chemical substance.

11. PISTON DISPLACEMENT — Volume displaced by piston as it travels length of stroke.

12. SAFETY PLUG — Device which releases the contents of a container above normal pressures, and before rupture pressures are reached.

13. HALIDE REFRIGERANTS — Family of refrigerants containing halogen chemicals.

14. INSULATION — Any material or substance which has the ability to retard the flow or transfer of heat.

15. PURGE UNIT — An independent refrigeration system that separates the non-condensables from the refrigerant and re-condenses and collects any refrigerant in the exhaust vent stream.

16. ECONIMIZER — A mechanism that removes flash gas from the evaporator.

17. EVAPORATOR — Evaporates low pressure vapor from the expansion device

18. GAS — The form of matter that is an easily compressible fluid

19. EBULATOR — A pointed or sharp edged solid substance inserted in flooded type evaporators to improve evaporation (boiling) of refrigerant in coil.

20. SAFETY CONTROL — Device used to electrically shut down a refrigerating unit when unsafe pressures and

21. HEAT — Invisible energy caused by the motion of molecules within any substance or matter.

22. EVAPORATOR COIL — Where heat is absorbed by warm air passing across. Liquid refrigerant boils as it is metered into coil, and changes from liquid to vapor.

23. HEAD PRESSURE — Pressure which exists in condensing side of refrigerating system.

24. AMPERE — Unit of measure referring to the flow of electrons within a circuit.

25. STORAGE CYLINDERS — Larger cylinders used for storing refrigerant to be transferred to smaller refillable cylinders.

A. Storage cylinders
B. Head Pressure
C. Insulation
D. Evaporator
E. Ebulator
F. Absorption Refrigerator
G. Econimizer
H. Ampere
I. Safety Control
J. Montreal Protocol
K. Purge unit
L. Very high pressure
M. Technician
N. Piston Displacement
O. Dehydration Evacuation
P. Halide Refrigerants
Q. Reusable cylinders
R. Gas
S. Evaporator Coil
T. Safety Plug
U. Volt
V. Ultraviolet Radiation
W. Opening
X. Recovery
Y. Heat

E. Provide the word that best matches each clue.

1. RECLAIM — Converting recycled refrigerant into a product to be reused.

2. CONDENSER COIL — Dissipates heat from the refrigerant.

3. GAUGE MANIFOLD — A tool that measures pressure readings at different points in the refrigeration system.

4. ACTIVATED CARBON — Specially processed carbon used as a filter drier; commonly used to clean air.

5. LIMIT CONTROL — Control used to open or close electrical circuits as temperature or pressure limits are reached.

6. FARAD — Unit of electrical capacity; capacity of a condenser which, when charged with one coulomb of electricity, gives difference of potential of one volt.

7. JOULE — Change in temperature of a gas on expansion through a porous plug from a high pressure to a lower pressure.

8. SATURATION TEMPERATURE — The temperature where a refrigerant exists in both liquid and vapor form relative to its measured pressure.

9. VACUUM PUMP — Special high efficiency device (pump) used create deep vacuum within an AC

10. THERM — Quantity of heat equivalent to 100,000 Btu.

11. EXPANSION DEVICE — Converts high pressure liquid to low pressure vapor

12. ECONIMIZER — A mechanism that removes flash gas from the evaporator.

13. VAPOR — Gas phase

14. SERVICE VALVE — Typically, a multi ported valve used by service technicians to isolate remote system components, as well as check pressures and charge refrigerating units.

15. MANOMETER — Instrument to measuring pressure of gases and vapors.

16. ABSOLUTE TEMPERATURE — A temperature scale in which the lowest temperature that can be attained theoretically is zero

17. SOLENOID VALVE — Valve actuated by magnetic action by means of an electrically energized coil.

18. LINE SET — The piping used to connect the outdoor unit to the indoor unit.

19. WAX — Undesirable component in many refrigeration lubricants, which may separate out of solution if cooled sufficiently.

20. VOLT — Electrical "pressure" applied to a circuit.

21. CHLORINE — The atom found in CFC and HCFC refrigerants that destroys ozone in the stratosphere.

22. ADSORBENT — Substance which has property to hold molecules of fluids without causing a chemical or physical change.

23. TEMPERATURE — Degree of hotness or coldness as measured by a thermometer

24. **ABSOLUTE TEMPERATURE**   Temperature measured from absolute zero.

25. **CAPACITANCE**   Property of non-conductor that permits storage of electrical energy in an electrostatic field.

A. Limit Control
B. Wax
C. Manometer
D. Therm
E. Absolute Temperature
F. Vapor
G. Service Valve
H. Vacuum Pump
I. Condenser Coil
J. Reclaim
K. Joule
L. Saturation Temperature
M. Absolute Temperature
N. Expansion device
O. Activated Carbon
P. Econimizer
Q. Solenoid Valve
R. Line Set
S. Adsorbent
T. Capacitance
U. Farad
V. Volt
W. Temperature
X. Gauge manifold
Y. Chlorine

F. Provide the word that best matches each clue.

1. **GAS**   Vapor phase or state of a substance.

2. **TEMPERATURE**   Degree of hotness or coldness as measured by a thermometer

3. **FAN**   A radial or axial flow device used for moving or producing artificial currents of air.

4. **CAPACITANCE**   Property of non-conductor that permits storage of electrical energy in an electrostatic field.

5. **FLAME TEST**   Tool which is principally a torch and when an air refrigerant mixture is fed to flame, this flame will change color in presence of heated copper.

6. **OHMMETER**   An instrument for measuring resistance in ohms.

7. **EBULATOR**   A pointed or sharp edged solid substance inserted in flooded type evaporators to improve evaporation (boiling) of refrigerant in coil.

8. **GAS**   The form of matter that is an easily compressible fluid

9. **SUPER HEAT**   The temperature rise within an evaporator or suction line assembly from the evaporator's saturation temperature.

10. **FILTER**   Device for removing small particles from a fluid.

11. **PARALLEL**   Side by side and having the same distance continuously between them.

12. **TON**   A unit of measurement used for determining cooling capacity. One ton is the equivalent of 12,000 BTUs per hour.

13. **HIGH PRESSURE**   A refrigerant has a boiling point between minus 50C and 10C degrees at atmospheric pressure.

14. DUCTWORK — Round or rectangular pipes or controlled paths acting as conduit for return, mixed, makeup, supply or exhaust air.

15. FRACTIONATION — A separation process in which a certain quantity of a mixture is divided during a phase transition

16. RUPTURE DISC — protects equipment or system from over pressurization or damaging vacuum conditions.

17. THERMOSTAT — A temperature control device. Typically mounted in conditioned space.

18. STATIC HEAD — Pressure of fluid expressed in terms of height of column of the fluid, such as water or mercury.

19. SAFETY CONTROL — Device used to electrically shut down a refrigerating unit when unsafe pressures and

20. ECONIMIZER — A mechanism that removes flash gas from the evaporator.

21. RECEIVER HEATING ELEMENT — Electrical resistance mounted in or around liquid receiver, used to maintain head pressures when ambient temperature is at freezing or below freezing.

22. WATT — Unit of electrical power.

23. CHLORINE — The atom found in CFC and HCFC refrigerants that destroys ozone in the stratosphere.

24. REUSABLE CYLINDERS — Gray cylinder with a yellow top; used for recovery or transporting refrigerant.

25. PSC MOTOR — High-efficiency design motor used on virtually all of today's HVAC & R equipment requiring motors.

A. Reusable cylinders	B. Econimizer	C. Gas
D. Temperature	E. Chlorine	F. Safety Control
G. Watt	H. Ebulator	I. Ductwork
J. Flame Test	K. Fractionation	L. Capacitance
M. Ohmmeter	N. Thermostat	O. Parallel
P. Receiver Heating Element	Q. Static Head	R. Gas
S. PSC Motor	T. TON	U. Super Heat
V. Rupture disc	W. High pressure	X. Fan
Y. Filter		

G. Provide the word that best matches each clue.

1. FAN — A radial or axial flow device used for moving or producing artificial currents of air.

2. INDUCTION MOTOR — An AC motor which operates on principle of rotating magnetic field. Rotor has no electrical connection, but receives electrical energy by transformer action from field windings.

3. VELOCITY HEAD — In flowing fluid, height of fluid equivalent to its velocity pressure.

4. VACUUM CONTROL SYSTEM — In some air conditioning systems, vacuum is used to operate dampers and controls in system.

5. ABSOLUTE PRESSURE — Gauge pressure plus atmospheric pressure (14.7 lbs. per sq. in.).

6. HALIDE TORCH — Type of torch used to detect halogen refrigerant leaks.

7. OZONE LAYER — Protective shield for Earth from the sun's harmful ultraviolet (UV) rays in the stratosphere layer that extends about 6 to 30 miles above earth.

8. LEAK RATE — The rate at which an appliance is losing refrigerant.

9. HUMIDITY — The total amount of moisture in air.

10. VACUUM GAUGE — Instrument used to measure pressures below atmospheric pressure.

11. SAFETY MOTOR CONTROL — Electrical device used to open circuit if the temperature, pressure, and

12. ABSOLUTE HUMIDITY — Amount of moisture in the air, indicated in grains per cubic foot.

13. EDDY CURRENTS — Induced currents flowing in a core.

14. VAPOR — Gas phase

15. MISCIBLE — Forming a homogeneous mixture of liquids when added together.

16. RANGE — Pressure or temperature settings of a control; change within limits.

17. OFF CYCLE — That time period of a refrigeration cycle when the system is not operating.

18. SAFETY CONTROL — Device used to electrically shut down a refrigerating unit when unsafe pressures and

19. ATMOSPHERE — A unit of Pressure equal to exactly 760 mmHg

20. RED — High Pressure

21. NITROGEN — Gas used for leak detection.

22. PISTON — Close fitting part which moves up and down in a cylinder.

23. BUBBLE POINT — The temperature at which the non-azeotropic blend first begins to evaporate.

24. GAS _____ The form of matter that is an easily compressible fluid

25. HEAD PRESSURE _____ Pressure which exists in condensing side of refrigerating system.

A. Piston	B. Head Pressure	C. Leak Rate
D. Humidity	E. Safety Motor Control	F. Velocity Head
G. Red	H. Vacuum Control System	I. Bubble Point
J. Vapor	K. Ozone layer	L. Gas
M. Vacuum Gauge	N. Range	O. Safety Control
P. Nitrogen	Q. Eddy Currents	R. Miscible
S. Induction Motor	T. Absolute Humidity	U. Atmosphere
V. Halide Torch	W. Fan	X. Absolute Pressure
Y. Off Cycle		

H. Provide the word that best matches each clue.

1. PURGE UNIT _____ An independent refrigeration system that separates the non-condensables from the refrigerant and re-condenses and collects any refrigerant in the exhaust vent stream.

2. WET BULB _____ Device used in measurement of relative humidity. Evaporation of moisture lowers temperature of wet bulb compared to dry bulb temperature in same area.

3. SERVICE MANIFOLD _____ A device equipped with gauges and manual valves, used by serviceman to service refrigerating systems.

4. VACUUM GAUGE _____ Instrument used to measure pressures below atmospheric pressure.

5. KELVIN _____ The SI base unit of temperature; a unit on an absolute temperature scale.

6. PARALLEL _____ Side by side and having the same distance continuously between them.

7. DENSITY _____ The mass per unit volume of a substance or solution.

8. KING VALVE _____ A combination shut-off and service value typically used on the inlet and outlet of a compressor.

9. HUMIDITY _____ The total amount of moisture in air.

10. BACK PRESSURE _____ Pressure in low side of refrigerating system; also called suction pressure or low side pressure.

11. HEAT EXCHANGER _____ A device for the transfer of heat energy from the source to the conveying medium, with the latter often being air or water.

12. EDDY CURRENTS _____ Induced currents flowing in a core.

13. CHLORINE _____ The atom found in CFC and HCFC refrigerants that destroys ozone in the stratosphere.

14. ACR TUBING   Tubing used in refrigeration which has ends to keep tubing clean and dry.

15. DEW POINT   The temperature at which the non-azeotropic blend first begins to condense.

16. ABSOLUTE TEMPERATURE   Temperature measured from absolute zero.

17. SUB COOLING   Process whereas additional sensible heat (as opposed to latent heat) is removed from condensed refrigerant liquid prior to the metering device.

18. HEAT   Invisible energy caused by the motion of molecules within any substance or matter.

19. GAS   The form of matter that is an easily compressible fluid

20. DE MINIMUS   Latin for the least amount of Refrigerant you can release into the atmosphere.

21. RECYCLE   To extract refrigerant from an appliance and clean refrigerant for reuse without meeting all of the requirements for reclamation.

22. CONDENSER   Condenses high pressure gas from the compressor to high pressure liquid.

23. CALORIMETER   Device used to measure quantities of heat or determine specific heats.

24. FILTER   Device for removing small particles from a fluid.

25. RUPTURE DISC   protects equipment or system from over pressurization or damaging vacuum conditions.

A. Rupture disc	B. Filter	C. Condenser
D. Gas	E. Eddy Currents	F. Density
G. Recycle	H. Calorimeter	I. Heat Exchanger
J. ACR Tubing	K. Service Manifold	L. De Minimus
M. Dew Point	N. Parallel	O. Sub Cooling
P. Purge unit	Q. King Valve	R. Absolute Temperature
S. Humidity	T. Vacuum Gauge	U. Chlorine
V. Kelvin	W. Back Pressure	X. Heat
Y. Wet Bulb		

Word Search

A. Find the hidden words. The words have been placed horizontally, vertically, or diagonally. When you locate a word, draw an ellipse around it.

I	G	A	C	T	I	V	E	R	E	C	O	V	E	R	Y	L	G	H	I	F	E	O
S	X	B	J	B	I	O	U	P	W	Z	L	O	W	P	R	E	S	S	U	R	E	S
N	V	D	O	H	N	L	Y	X	A	R	I	V	B	V	L	R	F	M	H	T	A	E
Q	I	A	U	J	G	W	B	J	X	X	B	A	D	S	O	R	P	T	I	O	N	D
I	T	R	L	I	E	Z	Y	P	U	R	G	E	U	N	I	T	V	J	L	O	W	T
R	C	Q	E	J	C	C	M	V	Y	N	X	M	C	Y	G	O	W	N	T	G	R	T
B	U	J	B	N	J	Y	R	T	C	V	O	L	T	T	H	E	R	M	M	H	R	E
H	G	S	G	V	O	H	T	E	S	T	L	I	G	H	T	I	S	O	L	A	T	E
A	J	F	T	W	C	A	L	A	T	E	N	T	H	E	A	T	R	H	M	X	U	P
L	C	Y	A	V	A	E	C	O	N	I	M	I	Z	E	R	B	O	D	X	H	U	U
O	D	I	S	P	O	S	A	B	L	E	C	Y	L	I	N	D	E	R	S	Z	V	G
N	C	H	E	H	Y	S	J	S	E	R	V	I	C	E	M	A	N	I	F	O	L	D
J	W	A	M	Z	N	R	R	M	I	C	R	O	N	E	V	H	X	F	T	D	L	R
E	G	K	K	C	K	Z	D	I	S	T	I	L	L	A	T	I	O	N	W	G	T	P
A	B	S	O	L	U	T	E	H	U	M	I	D	I	T	Y	Z	I	Q	W	W	S	O
D	U	N	C	B	M	A	C	R	T	U	B	I	N	G	P	A	R	A	L	L	E	L

1. Heat energy absorbed in process of changing form of substance without change in temperature or pressure.
2. Quantity of heat equivalent to 100,000 Btu.
3. Change in temperature of a gas on expansion through a porous plug from a high pressure to a lower pressure.
4. The action of purifying a liquid by a process of heating and cooling.
5. One thousandth of a millimeter.
6. An independent refrigeration system that separates the non-condensables from the refrigerant and re-condenses and collects any refrigerant in the exhaust vent stream.
7. Electrical "pressure" applied to a circuit.
8. A refrigerant has a boiling point above 10C or 50F at atmospheric pressure.
9. Light provided with test leads, used to test or probe electrical circuits to determine if they are alive.
10. Tubing used in refrigeration which has ends to keep tubing clean and dry.
11. A device equipped with gauges and manual valves, used by serviceman to service refrigerating systems.
12. Equipment that has its own compressor or pump.
13. Amount of moisture in the air, indicated in grains per cubic foot.
14. cause to be or remain alone or apart from others.
15. A mechanism that removes flash gas from the evaporator.
16. Undesirable component in many refrigeration lubricants, which may separate out of solution if cooled sufficiently.
17. Side by side and having the same distance continuously between them.
18. Single use cylinders. Empty cylinders should have the pressure reduced to zero and the cylinder rendered unusable.
19. The adhesion of a thin layer of molecules of a gas or liquid to a solid object.
20. A chemical used in fire extinguishing.

A. Latent Heat	B. Volt	C. Wax	D. Adsorption
E. Parallel	F. Test Light	G. Absolute Humidity	H. Micron
I. Halon	J. Isolate	K. ACR Tubing	L. Econimizer
M. Joule	N. Purge unit	O. Low pressure	P. Service Manifold
Q. Therm	R. Active recovery	S. Distillation	T. Disposable cylinders

B. Find the hidden words. The words have been placed horizontally, vertically, or diagonally. When you locate a word, draw an ellipse around it.

P	H	E	A	T	E	X	C	H	A	N	G	E	R	E	D	Y	R	D	S	R	K	R
A	B	S	O	L	U	T	E	Z	E	R	O	T	E	M	P	E	R	A	T	U	R	E
I	I	J	S	U	B	C	O	O	L	I	N	G	D	M	Q	E	I	W	O	C	M	Z
J	S	U	P	E	R	H	E	A	T	D	N	K	O	S	E	K	P	F	R	D	M	R
P	H	A	L	I	D	E	R	E	F	R	I	G	E	R	A	N	T	S	A	Q	G	D
O	M	I	S	O	L	A	T	E	C	D	S	L	C	F	H	E	A	T	G	T	A	B
R	E	C	E	I	V	E	R	H	E	A	T	I	N	G	E	L	E	M	E	N	T	B
Y	V	F	N	R	J	G	A	P	R	E	C	E	I	V	E	R	O	C	C	L	M	A
B	A	C	F	X	M	X	Z	X	F	H	P	R	E	S	S	U	R	E	Y	Q	J	V
Q	C	S	K	E	A	C	T	I	V	E	R	E	C	O	V	E	R	Y	L	U	S	D
I	U	R	A	P	M	U	I	J	R	E	F	R	I	G	E	R	A	T	I	O	N	Q
Q	U	O	M	B	P	O	H	M	Q	D	Q	J	X	I	H	C	B	E	N	S	X	X
I	M	N	P	I	E	F	J	P	S	C	M	O	T	O	R	I	T	J	D	R	B	K
B	P	D	D	O	R	J	D	I	S	T	I	L	L	A	T	I	O	N	E	G	L	Q
B	A	C	K	S	E	A	T	I	N	G	V	O	T	S	A	I	M	W	R	M	U	P
B	E	Y	D	S	C	A	L	I	B	R	A	T	E	M	V	T	H	L	S	E	E	D

1. Process whereas additional sensible heat (as opposed to latent heat) is removed from condensed refrigerant liquid prior to the metering device.
2. Invisible energy caused by the motion of molecules within any substance or matter.
3. cause to be or remain alone or apart from others.
4. The action of purifying a liquid by a process of heating and cooling.
5. Unit of measure referring to the flow of electrons within a circuit.
6. Larger cylinders used for storing refrigerant to be transferred to smaller refillable cylinders.
7. Electrical resistance mounted in or around liquid receiver, used to maintain head pressures when ambient temperature is at freezing or below freezing.
8. A standard unit of measure for electrical resistance.
9. High-efficiency design motor used on virtually all of today's HVAC & R equipment requiring motors.
10. Equipment that has its own compressor or pump.
11. The temperature rise within an evaporator or suction line assembly from the evaporator's saturation temperature.
12. Receives high pressure liquid from the condenser
13. Fluid opening
14. To determine; position indicators as required to obtain accurate measurements.
15. Temperature at which molecular motion ceases.
16. The force exerted per unit area of surface.
17. The process of cooling or chilling.
18. Reduction in pressure below atmospheric pressure.
19. A device for the transfer of heat energy from the source to the conveying medium, with the latter often being air or water.
20. Family of refrigerants containing halogen chemicals.
21. Low pressure

A. Blue
D. Ampere
G. Back Seating
J. Vacuum
M. Refrigeration
P. Receiver
S. Sub Cooling

B. Isolate
E. OHM
H. Heat
K. PSC Motor
N. Absolute Zero Temperature
Q. Distillation
T. Receiver Heating Element

C. Super Heat
F. Active recovery
I. Halide Refrigerants
L. Pressure
O. Storage cylinders
R. Heat Exchanger
U. Calibrate

C. Find the hidden words. The words have been placed horizontally, vertically, or diagonally. When you locate a word, draw an ellipse around it.

H	B	L	U	E	T	S	X	L	M	A	N	O	M	E	T	E	R	V	B	H	N	M
Z	L	S	A	G	C	U	G	K	L	R	O	I	N	P	C	S	V	U	O	T	Q	E
G	D	I	J	Z	U	P	T	U	T	E	C	H	N	I	C	I	A	N	R	D	H	V
P	A	S	S	I	V	E	R	E	C	O	V	E	R	Y	N	N	X	A	I	I	U	W
R	E	C	O	V	E	R	Y	B	D	F	W	N	O	S	V	Q	U	E	F	V	M	T
Z	G	N	W	I	S	H	H	K	Q	H	I	N	P	H	V	A	U	P	I	Q	I	O
T	V	U	Q	N	U	E	R	R	K	N	S	E	Q	X	B	D	P	S	C	Z	D	Q
O	P	A	R	T	I	A	L	P	R	E	S	S	U	R	E	I	A	C	E	M	I	K
W	X	I	Y	H	X	T	U	D	E	H	Y	D	R	A	T	E	V	M	P	E	T	P
R	E	C	Y	C	L	E	T	E	S	T	L	I	G	H	T	B	X	O	L	F	Y	Q
A	A	B	S	O	R	B	E	N	T	C	R	C	A	P	A	C	I	T	A	N	C	E
A	X	X	Y	D	R	P	N	D	G	B	E	B	F	S	J	J	U	O	T	Q	L	S
C	O	M	P	O	U	N	D	G	A	U	G	E	K	N	S	W	Z	R	E	A	W	D
Y	Y	Z	O	A	C	T	I	V	A	T	E	D	A	L	U	M	I	N	A	X	I	D
P	M	T	F	A	B	S	O	L	U	T	E	T	E	M	P	E	R	A	T	U	R	E
T	A	B	S	O	R	P	T	I	O	N	R	E	F	R	I	G	E	R	A	T	O	R

1. Requires the assistance of components such as the appliance or unit's compressor to remove the refrigerant from the appliance.
2. Property of non-conductor that permits storage of electrical energy in an electrostatic field.
3. To remove water from a system.
4. A passive throttling device, comprised of a small opening, located upstream of the evaporator.
5. The Pressure exerted by a particular Gas in a mixture.
6. Light provided with test leads, used to test or probe electrical circuits to determine if they are alive.
7. The temperature rise within an evaporator or suction line assembly from the evaporator's saturation temperature.
8. Instrument to measuring pressure of gases and vapors.
9. Any person who performs maintenance, service, or repair that could reasonably be expected to release class I or class II substances into the atmosphere.
10. Refrigerator which creates low temperatures by using the cooling effect formed when a refrigerant is absorbed by chemical substance.
11. The process of collecting used refrigerant.
12. Low pressure
13. The total amount of moisture in air.
14. Chemical used as a drier or desiccant.
15. High-efficiency design motor used on virtually all of today's HVAC & R equipment requiring motors.
16. Substance with ability to take up, or absorb another substance.
17. To extract refrigerant from an appliance and clean refrigerant for reuse without meeting all of the requirements for reclamation.
18. A temperature scale in which the lowest temperature that can be attained theoretically is zero
19. Measures low pressure and vacuum.

A. Absolute Temperature
E. Orifice Plate
I. Super Heat
M. PSC Motor
Q. Humidity

B. Absorption Refrigerator
F. Activated Alumina
J. Technician
N. Absorbent
R. Test Light

C. Blue
G. Manometer
K. Dehydrate
O. Compound gauge
S. Partial Pressure

D. Recycle
H. Capacitance
L. Passive recovery
P. Recovery

D. Find the hidden words. The words have been placed horizontally, vertically, or diagonally. When you locate a word, draw an ellipse around it.

W	T	K	N	Y	F	V	E	R	Y	H	I	G	H	P	R	E	S	S	U	R	E	A
R	M	K	C	U	A	R	B	B	O	V	C	G	N	N	L	Z	D	K	I	U	S	X
E	C	B	K	N	H	X	V	G	A	Q	I	G	I	L	Y	A	O	S	F	X	F	H
F	O	U	N	Q	H	A	L	I	D	E	R	E	F	R	I	G	E	R	A	N	T	S
R	H	B	B	N	Y	S	L	U	G	D	P	K	I	O	H	S	G	T	O	H	M	T
I	M	B	C	G	V	U	N	F	E	V	A	P	O	R	A	T	O	R	C	O	I	L
G	M	L	H	V	U	P	A	E	N	I	T	R	O	G	E	N	B	N	Y	P	S	C
E	E	E	L	A	X	E	M	A	C	T	I	V	E	R	E	C	O	V	E	R	Y	Q
R	T	P	O	P	O	R	U	M	T	Z	J	M	T	N	S	V	A	W	Q	I	H	Y
A	E	O	R	O	L	H	R	K	F	I	E	L	D	P	O	L	E	T	I	V	B	I
T	R	I	I	R	W	E	X	V	R	K	M	N	V	Y	S	Y	U	Z	T	W	I	U
I	S	N	N	B	F	A	E	F	W	Q	D	E	M	I	N	I	M	U	S	I	T	R
O	F	T	E	C	W	T	G	Y	S	A	F	E	T	Y	C	O	N	T	R	O	L	L
N	L	A	M	P	E	R	E	D	M	R	B	C	F	H	E	Y	X	K	M	Y	R	U
B	D	E	H	Y	D	R	A	T	E	Z	Q	U	W	D	R	B	E	J	Q	V	H	S
C	M	Z	J	O	Q	S	T	A	T	I	C	H	E	A	D	K	R	S	Q	V	X	A

1. Equipment that has its own compressor or pump.
2. Unit of measure referring to the flow of electrons within a circuit.
3. The temperature rise within an evaporator or suction line assembly from the evaporator's saturation temperature.
4. To remove water from a system.
5. Where heat is absorbed by warm air passing across. Liquid refrigerant boils as it is metered into coil, and changes from liquid to vapor.
6. An instrument for measuring resistance in ohms.
7. A refrigerant has a boiling point below minus 50C or minus 58F at atmospheric pressure.
8. The Gaseous state of any kind of matter that normally exists as a liquid or solid.
9. The atom found in CFC and HCFC refrigerants that destroys ozone in the stratosphere.
10. The moving of heat from an undesirable location, to that of a location where its presence is less undesirable.
11. Device used to electrically shut down a refrigerating unit when unsafe pressures and
12. Latin for the least amount of Refrigerant you can release into the atmosphere.
13. The temperature at which the non-azeotropic blend first begins to evaporate.
14. Family of refrigerants containing halogen chemicals.
15. Gas used for leak detection.
16. Part of stator of motor which concentrates magnetic field of field winding.
17. A standard unit of measure for electrical resistance.
18. Pressure of fluid expressed in terms of height of column of the fluid, such as water or mercury.

A. Evaporator Coil
E. Bubble Point
I. Safety Control
M. OHM
Q. Dehydrate

B. Very high pressure
F. Chlorine
J. Nitrogen
N. Super Heat
R. Vapor

C. De Minimus
G. Halide Refrigerants
K. Static Head
O. Ohmmeter

D. Active recovery
H. Refrigeration
L. Ampere
P. Field Pole

E. Find the hidden words. The words have been placed horizontally, vertically, or diagonally. When you locate a word, draw an ellipse around it.

B	U	N	C	T	H	E	R	M	L	D	D	J	Q	M	I	B	Y	V	J	D	N	V
R	G	E	O	V	G	H	O	N	Y	D	E	H	Y	D	R	A	T	E	K	Y	A	O
E	A	U	N	D	T	B	E	X	P	A	N	S	I	O	N	D	E	V	I	C	E	Q
C	U	T	D	L	Z	J	Y	T	T	A	B	J	X	F	K	I	S	T	E	N	R	N
O	G	R	E	A	Q	V	K	S	A	F	E	T	Y	C	O	N	T	R	O	L	V	P
V	E	A	N	B	C	J	M	D	P	G	W	L	S	Q	Z	L	A	K	K	A	T	A
E	M	L	S	H	I	G	H	P	R	E	S	S	U	R	E	V	T	U	W	T	J	C
R	A	I	E	A	B	S	O	L	U	T	E	H	U	M	I	D	I	T	Y	M	I	C
Y	N	Z	R	M	I	C	R	O	N	R	E	C	L	A	I	M	C	C	Q	O	R	U
T	I	E	M	S	U	B	C	O	O	L	I	N	G	W	Q	T	H	K	V	S	A	M
D	F	R	T	P	I	S	T	O	N	X	R	K	N	X	T	R	E	I	Z	P	Q	U
M	O	N	T	R	E	A	L	P	R	O	T	O	C	O	L	C	A	F	B	H	H	L
D	L	G	V	A	N	M	G	Y	M	R	T	Q	T	P	C	A	D	W	P	E	V	A
R	D	B	R	I	T	I	S	H	T	H	E	R	M	A	L	U	N	I	T	R	N	T
T	I	I	W	D	N	I	T	R	O	G	E	N	R	Z	D	Z	P	N	L	E	O	O
M	N	H	A	L	I	D	E	R	E	F	R	I	G	E	R	A	N	T	S	P	U	R

1. Treaty among nations designed to protect the stratospheric ozone layer.
2. A unit of Pressure equal to exactly 760 mmHg
3. Close fitting part which moves up and down in a cylinder.
4. Condenses high pressure gas from the compressor to high pressure liquid.
5. One thousandth of a millimeter.
6. Pressure of fluid expressed in terms of height of column of the fluid, such as water or mercury.
7. Substance used to counteract acids, in refrigeration system.
8. Quantity of heat equivalent to 100,000 Btu.
9. Amount of moisture in the air, indicated in grains per cubic foot.
10. A refrigerant has a boiling point between minus 50C and 10C degrees at atmospheric pressure.
11. Device used to electrically shut down a refrigerating unit when unsafe pressures and

12. A tool that measures pressure readings at different points in the refrigeration system.
13. Converting recycled refrigerant into a product to be reused.
14. Gas used for leak detection.
15. Family of refrigerants containing halogen chemicals.
16. To remove water from a system.
17. Represents the amount of energy required to raise one pound of water one degree Fahrenheit.
18. Converts high pressure liquid to low pressure vapor
19. The process of collecting used refrigerant.
20. Accumulates any low pressure liquid from the evaporator so it can vaporize before entering the compressor
21. Process whereas additional sensible heat (as opposed to latent heat) is removed from condensed refrigerant liquid prior to the metering device.

A. Reclaim
E. Halide Refrigerants
I. Gauge manifold
M. Dehydrate
Q. High pressure
U. Piston

B. Accumulator
F. Neutralizer
J. Safety Control
N. Expansion device
R. Therm

C. Micron
G. Recovery
K. Static Head
O. Sub Cooling
S. British Thermal Unit

D. Nitrogen
H. Absolute Humidity
L. Condenser
P. Atmosphere
T. Montreal Protocol

F. Find the hidden words. The words have been placed horizontally, vertically, or diagonally. When you locate a word, draw an ellipse around it.

W	G	N	L	K	O	A	R	T	J	D	C	E	V	A	P	O	R	A	T	O	R	D
X	B	Z	O	F	H	Y	D	R	O	S	T	A	T	I	C	N	W	V	G	P	W	X
H	I	G	H	P	R	E	S	S	U	R	E	O	D	J	X	T	B	U	S	X	W	F
O	Z	O	N	E	L	A	Y	E	R	R	E	F	R	I	G	E	R	A	N	T	X	U
A	B	S	O	L	U	T	E	T	E	M	P	E	R	A	T	U	R	E	D	P	T	P
U	L	T	R	A	V	I	O	L	E	T	R	A	D	I	A	T	I	O	N	T	U	M
I	D	W	G	J	F	Y	R	Y	O	D	D	P	R	Q	O	V	K	R	T	E	Z	H
J	J	F	A	W	C	T	C	X	C	G	E	M	D	C	O	L	D	O	T	M	S	X
R	E	F	R	I	G	E	R	A	N	T	C	I	R	C	U	I	T	Z	S	P	V	K
W	S	T	O	R	A	G	E	C	Y	L	I	N	D	E	R	S	E	T	H	E	O	G
S	A	D	D	L	E	V	A	L	V	E	B	G	H	E	C	V	U	E	Z	R	U	Q
D	E	W	P	O	I	N	T	F	N	C	E	F	O	D	E	H	Y	D	R	A	T	E
A	C	E	N	T	E	R	P	O	R	T	L	L	W	C	O	C	U	D	N	T	R	B
E	X	M	F	M	T	H	V	H	Y	D	R	O	C	A	R	B	O	N	M	U	V	S
A	K	A	C	T	I	V	A	T	E	D	C	A	R	B	O	N	S	Y	O	R	Z	B
V	A	P	O	R	P	A	R	T	I	A	L	P	R	E	S	S	U	R	E	E	S	L

1. Unit used for measuring relative loudness of sounds.
2. Degree of hotness or coldness as measured by a thermometer
3. The temperature at which the non-azeotropic blend first begins to condense.
4. Breaks down the CFCs and frees the chlorine ion at stratosphere.
5. A form of testing for high pressure cylinders.
6. Specially processed carbon used as a filter drier; commonly used to clean air.
7. A refrigerant has a boiling point between minus 50C and 10C degrees at atmospheric pressure.
8. To remove water from a system.
9. The Gaseous state of any kind of matter that normally exists as a liquid or solid.
10. The Pressure exerted by a particular Gas in a mixture.
11. A substance produces a refrigerating or cooling effect while expanding or vaporizing.
12. The parts of an appliance that are normally connected to each other and are designed to contain refrigerant.
13. Larger cylinders used for storing refrigerant to be transferred to smaller refillable cylinders.
14. Protective shield for Earth from the sun's harmful ultraviolet (UV) rays in the stratosphere layer that extends about 6 to 30 miles above earth.
15. Temperature measured from absolute zero.
16. Connects manifold to recovery device.
17. Self piercing valve body designed to be permanently silver brazed or clamped to refrigerant tubing surface.
18. A sensation felt as a result of the absence of heat.
19. Evaporates low pressure vapor from the expansion device
20. A compound containing only the elements hydrogen and carbon.

A. Cold
E. High pressure
I. Dew Point
M. Hydrostatic
Q. Activated Carbon

B. Ozone layer
F. Saddle Valve
J. Dehydrate
N. Temperature
R. Center port

C. Refrigerant
G. Decibel
K. Vapor
O. Hydrocarbon
S. Partial Pressure

D. Evaporator
H. Ultraviolet Radiation
L. Refrigerant circuit
P. Absolute Temperature
T. Storage cylinders

G. Find the hidden words. The words have been placed horizontally, vertically, or diagonally. When you locate a word, draw an ellipse around it.

L	M	O	D	I	S	P	O	S	A	B	L	E	C	Y	L	I	N	D	E	R	S	L
B	U	H	X	M	P	E	I	O	C	A	L	C	I	U	M	S	U	L	F	A	T	E
C	G	I	Q	F	P	I	O	E	J	Q	L	Y	F	G	K	S	Z	Q	A	E	Y	M
A	J	B	R	M	F	W	M	P	R	C	S	C	O	M	P	R	E	S	S	O	R	S
P	U	E	S	M	A	L	L	A	P	P	L	I	A	N	C	E	Z	G	Z	O	G	F
A	N	D	E	C	I	B	E	L	P	Q	B	V	D	M	V	N	X	E	M	Y	E	D
C	C	Q	U	H	Y	S	K	M	T	E	C	H	N	I	C	I	A	N	C	C	O	S
I	T	O	S	F	A	T	M	O	S	P	H	E	R	E	B	H	D	S	L	O	J	U
T	I	D	E	N	S	I	T	Y	P	A	S	C	A	L	S	L	A	W	P	M	H	K
A	O	A	B	S	O	L	U	T	E	P	R	E	S	S	U	R	E	F	O	P	Z	K
N	N	I	P	L	F	D	O	P	O	F	Z	B	V	W	M	F	S	N	B	O	J	G
C	B	K	G	T	G	M	B	O	J	O	I	J	B	I	A	K	S	Z	U	E	M
E	O	S	A	F	E	T	Y	C	O	N	T	R	O	L	C	R	D	M	L	N	E	Q
N	X	C	P	R	E	S	S	U	R	E	D	R	P	M	R	A	C	B	G	D	B	Y
D	S	M	I	S	C	I	B	L	E	Q	B	V	Y	D	O	D	O	E	A	F	V	Y
Q	D	W	O	A	Y	W	V	G	Q	G	D	Q	V	M	N	B	H	M	C	H	C	H

1. Group of electrical terminals housed in protective box or container.
2. Any products that are fully manufactured, charged, and hermetically sealed in a factory with five pounds or less of refrigerant
3. Any person who performs maintenance, service, or repair that could reasonably be expected to release class I or class II substances into the atmosphere.
4. Device used to electrically shut down a refrigerating unit when unsafe pressures and
5. Property of non-conductor that permits storage of electrical energy in an electrostatic field.
6. A substance formed by a union of two or more elements
7. Gauge pressure plus atmospheric pressure (14.7 lbs. per sq. in.).
8. One thousandth of a millimeter.
9. Unit used for measuring relative loudness of sounds.
10. The force exerted per unit area of surface.
11. A pressure imposed upon a fluid is transmitted equally in all directions.
12. The heart or "pump" within an air conditioning or heat pump system.
13. The mass per unit volume of a substance or solution.
14. Single use cylinders. Empty cylinders should have the pressure reduced to zero and the cylinder rendered unusable.
15. Forming a homogeneous mixture of liquids when added together.
16. Chemical compound which is used as a drying agent or desiccant in liquid line filter dryers.
17. Unit of electrical capacity; capacity of a condenser which, when charged with one coulomb of electricity, gives difference of potential of one volt.
18. A unit of Pressure equal to exactly 760 mmHg

A. Miscible
B. Decibel
C. Farad
D. Junction Box
E. Compressor
F. Calcium Sulfate
G. Pascals Law
H. Disposable cylinders
I. Atmosphere
J. Micron
K. Density
L. Pressure
M. Small appliance
N. Capacitance
O. Absolute Pressure
P. Technician
Q. Safety Control
R. Compound

H. Find the hidden words. The words have been placed horizontally, vertically, or diagonally. When you locate a word, draw an ellipse around it.

Z	J	C	Q	F	J	W	Z	P	S	Y	C	H	R	O	M	E	T	E	R	Q	H	G
E	A	L	C	O	L	D	Q	N	B	I	F	D	X	C	K	Y	F	D	R	N	X	N
D	O	V	J	D	N	M	K	S	N	Z	G	Z	Z	W	L	U	A	L	U	L	H	U
B	A	Z	J	X	Z	E	C	A	L	O	R	I	M	E	T	E	R	L	B	R	A	J
C	D	C	D	A	S	J	L	E	A	K	D	E	T	E	C	T	O	R	Q	I	L	C
A	S	R	P	C	A	S	O	O	F	F	C	Y	C	L	E	D	Q	C	K	B	I	T
J	O	R	B	C	T	C	H	B	U	B	B	L	E	P	O	I	N	T	C	J	D	M
W	R	Z	G	U	M	O	M	I	Y	R	C	O	M	P	R	E	S	S	O	R	E	V
Q	B	D	X	M	O	V	M	E	A	Z	E	O	T	R	O	P	H	C	D	R	T	J
T	E	U	F	U	S	J	E	V	T	U	O	R	E	C	O	V	E	R	Y	D	O	R
S	N	A	H	L	P	Z	T	P	A	R	T	I	A	L	P	R	E	S	S	U	R	E
A	T	U	G	A	H	M	E	R	C	O	S	S	X	W	N	M	F	P	W	R	C	F
Z	S	J	H	T	E	E	R	D	C	H	A	R	L	E	S	L	A	W	B	G	H	L
Z	F	H	Z	O	R	V	I	E	X	B	Y	Q	M	P	U	A	C	H	M	H	G	P
Y	G	Z	M	R	E	A	E	X	P	A	N	S	I	O	N	D	E	V	I	C	E	P
Q	S	A	B	S	O	L	U	T	E	T	E	M	P	E	R	A	T	U	R	E	Q	C

1. An instrument for measuring resistance in ohms.
2. Type of torch used to detect halogen refrigerant leaks.
3. A unit of Pressure equal to exactly 760 mmHg
4. The temperature at which the non-azeotropic blend first begins to evaporate.
5. The Pressure exerted by a particular Gas in a mixture.
6. Device used to measure quantities of heat or determine specific heats.
7. Device or instrument such as a halide torch, an electronic sniffer; or soap solution used to detect leaks.
8. A mixture of at least two different liquids.
9. Either a sling type, or electronic. Instrument used to determine wet bulb temperatures and relative humidity.
10. A sensation felt as a result of the absence of heat.
11. The process of collecting used refrigerant.
12. States that the volume occupied by a gas at a constant Pressure is directly proportional to the absolute temperature.
13. Converts high pressure liquid to low pressure vapor
14. Substance which has property to hold molecules of fluids without causing a chemical or physical change.
15. The heart or "pump" within an air conditioning or heat pump system.
16. Temperature measured from absolute zero.
17. Accumulates any low pressure liquid from the evaporator so it can vaporize before entering the compressor
18. That time period of a refrigeration cycle when the system is not operating.

A. Azeotroph
B. Halide Torch
C. Accumulator
D. Bubble Point
E. Leak Detector
F. Cold
G. Psychrometer
H. Off Cycle
I. Ohmmeter
J. Absolute Temperature
K. Recovery
L. Partial Pressure
M. Atmosphere
N. Compressor
O. Expansion device
P. Adsorbent
Q. Charles Law
R. Calorimeter

I. Find the hidden words. The words have been placed horizontally, vertically, or diagonally. When you locate a word, draw an ellipse around it.

L	L	R	G	A	U	G	E	M	A	N	I	F	O	L	D	D	E	C	I	B	E	L
Q	O	E	N	K	R	Y	A	C	H	A	R	L	E	S	L	A	W	F	I	I	O	Y
B	T	F	J	X	E	V	I	F	W	Q	T	Z	W	B	Y	H	M	V	S	N	E	K
V	E	R	B	Y	C	A	C	O	M	P	R	E	S	S	O	R	G	N	R	I	L	B
X	G	I	K	H	Y	P	P	S	Y	C	H	R	O	M	E	T	E	R	Y	T	Q	R
H	M	G	T	M	C	O	S	L	U	N	O	A	C	R	T	U	B	I	N	G	C	M
F	M	E	V	D	L	R	D	D	W	S	K	R	E	V	A	C	U	A	T	I	O	N
V	O	R	N	E	E	R	T	E	M	P	E	R	A	T	U	R	E	G	L	I	D	E
C	P	A	Q	R	J	S	E	A	F	R	R	I	M	Q	E	S	Y	O	W	A	G	M
P	C	T	D	G	D	B	B	G	A	M	Y	F	H	A	I	F	W	X	T	M	T	I
O	R	I	F	I	C	E	P	L	A	T	E	B	M	P	B	L	U	E	L	P	M	S
U	K	O	C	G	Y	W	Z	R	Y	C	Z	L	J	N	H	Q	Y	A	T	E	T	C
L	B	N	L	H	Z	W	P	A	R	A	L	L	E	L	B	U	C	E	C	R	N	I
R	U	I	R	Z	Z	C	P	Y	O	J	Y	J	T	N	J	M	C	D	L	E	V	B
S	A	T	H	U	M	I	D	I	T	Y	Y	Y	V	G	C	V	E	O	T	Z	M	U	L
A	B	S	O	L	U	T	E	Z	E	R	O	T	E	M	P	E	R	A	T	U	R	E

1. The difference between the Dew Point and the Bubble Point.
2. Reducing contaminants in the used refrigerant
3. A passive throttling device, comprised of a small opening, located upstream of the evaporator.
4. The heart or "pump" within an air conditioning or heat pump system.
5. States that the volume occupied by a gas at a constant Pressure is directly proportional to the absolute temperature.
6. Unit used for measuring relative loudness of sounds.
7. Unit of measure referring to the flow of electrons within a circuit.
8. Either a sling type, or electronic. Instrument used to determine wet bulb temperatures and relative humidity.
9. The moving of heat from an undesirable location, to that of a location where its presence is less undesirable.
10. The process of extracting any air, non-condensable gases, or water from the system.
11. Tubing used in refrigeration which has ends to keep tubing clean and dry.
12. The total amount of moisture in air.
13. Side by side and having the same distance continuously between them.
14. Low pressure
15. A tool that measures pressure readings at different points in the refrigeration system.
16. Temperature at which molecular motion ceases.
17. The Gaseous state of any kind of matter that normally exists as a liquid or solid.
18. Forming a homogeneous mixture of liquids when added together.

A. Gauge manifold
D. Charles Law
G. Parallel
J. Refrigeration
M. Blue
P. Recycle

B. Absolute Zero Temperature
E. Decibel
H. Compressor
K. Psychrometer
N. Vapor
Q. ACR Tubing

C. Orifice Plate
F. Ampere
I. Miscible
L. Humidity
O. Temperature Glide
R. Evacuation

J. Find the hidden words. The words have been placed horizontally, vertically, or diagonally. When you locate a word, draw an ellipse around it.

D	I	S	T	I	L	L	A	T	I	O	N	P	E	P	R	V	Y	X	D	V	M	I
X	S	N	X	G	J	L	A	T	E	N	T	H	E	A	T	E	S	I	Z	B	A	N
P	Q	R	G	A	S	Z	U	P	T	E	S	A	U	T	A	L	P	Y	X	Y	N	S
I	F	X	E	W	L	P	A	S	S	I	V	E	R	E	C	O	V	E	R	Y	O	U
N	L	E	O	S	G	X	D	B	K	X	A	T	C	W	O	C	S	I	U	U	M	L
C	A	U	P	W	A	N	F	X	J	B	X	C	P	A	H	I	L	O	M	O	E	A
H	M	W	C	Z	S	R	E	F	R	I	G	E	R	A	N	T	C	R	N	I	T	T
O	E	H	S	G	A	C	C	U	M	U	L	A	T	O	R	Y	R	X	L	W	E	I
F	T	P	C	S	A	F	E	T	Y	P	L	U	G	D	D	H	O	Z	Y	Y	R	O
F	E	Q	I	V	G	Y	V	W	T	B	A	C	K	P	R	E	S	S	U	R	E	N
T	S	H	O	J	Z	V	F	V	S	D	B	O	F	N	Q	A	R	D	L	G	Z	T
O	T	S	E	R	V	I	C	E	M	A	N	I	F	O	L	D	Y	D	I	Z	M	H
O	H	E	A	D	P	R	E	S	S	U	R	E	C	O	N	T	R	O	L	Q	Y	E
L	M	Q	G	L	P	M	K	Y	Y	D	N	M	B	K	H	L	Z	N	K	S	L	R
S	A	T	U	R	A	T	I	O	N	T	E	M	P	E	R	A	T	U	R	E	Z	M
R	S	U	S	W	Y	P	Z	P	X	J	X	T	E	M	S	M	B	U	O	R	N	P

1. Heat energy absorbed in process of changing form of substance without change in temperature or pressure.
2. In flowing fluid, height of fluid equivalent to its velocity pressure.
3. Quantity of heat equivalent to 100,000 Btu.
4. Tool which is principally a torch and when an air refrigerant mixture is fed to flame, this flame will change color in presence of heated copper.
5. The form of matter that is an easily compressible fluid
6. Requires the assistance of components such as the appliance or unit's compressor to remove the refrigerant from the appliance.
7. Pressure operated control which opens electrical circuit if high side pressure becomes excessive.
8. Pressure in low side of refrigerating system; also called suction pressure or low side pressure.
9. The action of purifying a liquid by a process of heating and cooling.
10. The temperature where a refrigerant exists in both liquid and vapor form relative to its measured pressure.

11. Vapor phase or state of a substance.
12. Device used to press walls of a tubing together until fluid flow ceases.
13. A device equipped with gauges and manual valves, used by serviceman to service refrigerating systems.
14. Instrument to measuring pressure of gases and vapors.
15. The fluid used for heat transfer in a refrigeration system, which absorbs heat during evaporation at low temperature and pressure, and releases heat during condensation.
16. Any material or substance which has the ability to retard the flow or transfer of heat.
17. Device which releases the contents of a container above normal pressures, and before rupture pressures are reached.
18. Accumulates any low pressure liquid from the evaporator so it can vaporize before entering the compressor

A. Refrigerant
D. Gas
G. Distillation
J. Manometer
M. Saturation Temperature
P. Gas

B. Therm
E. Pinch off Tool
H. Insulation
K. Accumulator
N. Latent Heat
Q. Velocity Head

C. Back Pressure
F. Flame Test
I. Safety Plug
L. Service Manifold
O. Head Pressure Control
R. Passive recovery

K. Find the hidden words. The words have been placed horizontally, vertically, or diagonally. When you locate a word, draw an ellipse around it.

Z	E	A	D	I	A	B	A	T	I	C	C	O	M	P	R	E	S	S	I	O	N	O
Q	H	A	L	I	D	E	R	E	F	R	I	G	E	R	A	N	T	S	S	I	M	C
X	N	N	Y	O	Q	M	E	T	E	R	I	N	G	D	E	V	I	C	E	W	Q	M
J	A	C	C	U	M	U	L	A	T	O	R	Z	O	Q	C	E	R	C	Y	G	B	I
A	B	S	O	L	U	T	E	P	R	E	S	S	U	R	E	X	W	H	D	E	C	V
A	A	V	E	L	O	C	I	T	Y	H	E	A	D	V	N	H	H	X	I	R	D	U
B	C	L	H	S	K	F	F	Y	C	P	L	I	F	A	S	Z	Z	W	F	A	X	N
S	C	T	U	T	B	K	T	A	Q	F	U	L	U	P	I	J	F	M	F	H	L	V
O	E	R	M	A	U	L	X	A	E	L	X	P	Q	O	O	E	D	Z	U	N	J	T
R	L	D	I	T	P	S	B	L	T	A	L	M	H	R	G	B	C	T	S	L	O	D
B	E	F	D	I	F	M	E	X	P	A	N	S	I	O	N	D	E	V	I	C	E	Q
E	R	S	I	C	X	Z	V	C	H	A	R	L	E	S	L	A	W	K	O	Z	Q	P
N	A	I	T	H	V	V	Z	M	N	I	T	R	O	G	E	N	I	S	N	S	T	F
T	T	A	Y	E	L	M	O	W	F	R	E	F	R	I	G	E	R	A	N	T	V	N
X	E	D	Q	A	Z	T	H	X	A	C	I	D	C	O	N	D	I	T	I	O	N	C
K	R	T	G	D	A	S	M	A	L	L	A	P	P	L	I	A	N	C	E	T	J	V

1. In flowing fluid, height of fluid equivalent to its velocity pressure.
2. Creates pressure drop to allow liquid refrigerant to boil and absorb latent heat.
3. Pressure of fluid expressed in terms of height of column of the fluid, such as water or mercury.
4. The total amount of moisture in air.
5. The process whereby a gas spreads out through another gas to occupy the space with uniform partial Pressure.
6. Condition in which refrigerant and
7. Gas used for leak detection.
8. The Gaseous state of any kind of matter that normally exists as a liquid or solid.
9. Storage tank which receives liquid refrigerant from evaporator and prevents it from flowing into suction line.
10. States that the volume occupied by a gas at a constant Pressure is directly proportional to the absolute temperature.
11. A substance produces a refrigerating or cooling effect while expanding or vaporizing.
12. Family of refrigerants containing halogen chemicals.
13. Substance with ability to take up, or absorb another substance.
14. Gauge pressure plus atmospheric pressure (14.7 lbs. per sq. in.).
15. Converts high pressure liquid to low pressure vapor
16. Any products that are fully manufactured, charged, and hermetically sealed in a factory with five pounds or less of refrigerant
17. Compressing refrigerant gas without removing or adding heat.
18. To add to speed; hasten progress of development.

A. Accelerate
E. Diffusion
I. Adiabatic Compression
M. Accumulator
Q. Expansion device

B. Absorbent
F. Metering Device
J. Acid Condition
N. Halide Refrigerants
R. Small appliance

C. Humidity
G. Nitrogen
K. Velocity Head
O. Refrigerant

D. Absolute Pressure
H. Vapor
L. Static Head
P. Charles Law

L. Find the hidden words. The words have been placed horizontally, vertically, or diagonally. When you locate a word, draw an ellipse around it.

D	M	L	C	P	K	S	V	S	M	A	L	L	A	P	P	L	I	A	N	C	E	J
Z	P	E	B	E	E	B	T	Z	X	C	N	Z	I	B	N	C	K	Y	A	Z	N	F
H	A	B	Q	K	J	U	T	X	R	E	F	R	I	G	E	R	A	T	I	O	N	N
L	S	V	A	D	I	A	B	A	T	I	C	C	O	M	P	R	E	S	S	I	O	N
Q	S	U	C	V	X	G	Q	Z	G	D	Q	V	V	U	K	X	Z	F	M	R	V	W
T	I	U	R	E	C	O	V	E	R	Y	E	C	O	N	I	M	I	Z	E	R	X	Z
E	V	T	E	M	P	E	R	A	T	U	R	E	G	L	I	D	E	N	T	R	Y	G
S	E	D	Z	P	O	H	M	M	E	T	E	R	C	E	O	F	F	C	Y	C	L	E
T	R	I	S	H	K	T	H	E	R	M	O	S	T	A	T	G	M	R	K	A	G	O
L	E	F	C	Q	S	T	O	R	A	G	E	C	Y	L	I	N	D	E	R	S	F	P
I	C	F	U	Q	Z	W	T	S	B	T	H	E	A	D	P	R	E	S	S	U	R	E
G	O	U	Z	U	Z	F	I	N	D	U	C	T	I	O	N	M	O	T	O	R	W	N
H	V	S	J	N	Y	B	A	D	B	T	R	C	D	N	S	T	U	G	V	P	S	I
T	E	I	G	T	M	O	N	T	R	E	A	L	P	R	O	T	O	C	O	L	T	N
D	R	O	S	C	M	H	N	I	E	Y	H	E	K	C	E	L	Z	F	Y	O	M	G
C	Y	N	N	W	A	T	M	O	S	P	H	E	R	E	J	B	Z	G	M	E	E	H

1. An instrument for measuring resistance in ohms.
2. Compressing refrigerant gas without removing or adding heat.
3. A temperature control device. Typically mounted in conditioned space.
4. Pressure which exists in condensing side of refrigerating system.
5. The difference between the Dew Point and the Bubble Point.
6. Larger cylinders used for storing refrigerant to be transferred to smaller refillable cylinders.
7. An AC motor which operates on principle of rotating magnetic field. Rotor has no electrical connection, but receives electrical energy by transformer action from field windings.
8. The process whereby a gas spreads out through another gas to occupy the space with uniform partial Pressure.
9. Light provided with test leads, used to test or probe electrical circuits to determine if they are alive.
10. Treaty among nations designed to protect the stratospheric ozone layer.
11. Any products that are fully manufactured, charged, and hermetically sealed in a factory with five pounds or less of refrigerant
12. A mechanism that removes flash gas from the evaporator.
13. Requires the assistance of components such as the appliance or unit's compressor to remove the refrigerant from the appliance.
14. The process of collecting used refrigerant.
15. A unit of Pressure equal to exactly 760 mmHg
16. That time period of a refrigeration cycle when the system is not operating.
17. Any maintenance or repair on an appliance that would release refrigerant from the appliance to the atmosphere.
18. The process of cooling or chilling.

A. Passive recovery
B. Head Pressure
C. Test Light
D. Thermostat
E. Econimizer
F. Induction Motor
G. Storage cylinders
H. Small appliance
I. Ohmmeter
J. Refrigeration
K. Opening
L. Temperature Glide
M. Atmosphere
N. Recovery
O. Off Cycle
P. Montreal Protocol
Q. Adiabatic Compression
R. Diffusion

121

M. Find the hidden words. The words have been placed horizontally, vertically, or diagonally. When you locate a word, draw an ellipse around it.

Y	C	Q	D	I	S	P	O	S	A	B	L	E	C	Y	L	I	N	D	E	R	S	O
K	G	H	Y	D	R	O	S	T	A	T	I	C	Z	O	V	O	K	N	E	V	I	F
A	H	Q	C	H	L	O	R	I	N	E	Q	V	W	J	T	S	H	Q	P	W	S	F
Z	K	I	T	E	M	P	E	R	A	T	U	R	E	G	L	I	D	E	H	W	Z	C
E	T	A	F	I	F	R	A	C	T	I	O	N	A	T	I	O	N	L	U	F	A	Y
O	R	C	A	B	P	J	A	A	T	I	Q	R	I	V	N	G	V	A	U	K	G	C
T	D	N	G	O	N	K	U	C	Z	F	V	Q	W	S	R	R	F	A	G	V	S	L
R	T	E	S	T	L	I	G	H	T	Q	Z	Q	F	E	F	F	U	S	I	O	N	E
O	S	M	A	L	L	A	P	P	L	I	A	N	C	E	R	Y	N	Z	M	K	Z	U
P	T	N	P	V	A	C	U	U	M	C	O	N	T	R	O	L	S	Y	S	T	E	M
H	S	A	T	U	R	A	T	I	O	N	T	E	M	P	E	R	A	T	U	R	E	T
R	E	F	R	I	G	E	R	A	T	I	O	N	N	C	O	H	M	M	E	T	E	R
A	B	S	O	L	U	T	E	Z	E	R	O	T	E	M	P	E	R	A	T	U	R	E
Y	G	X	V	A	C	U	U	M	P	U	M	P	U	D	U	B	L	C	W	P	Q	A
R	E	C	E	I	V	E	R	H	E	A	T	I	N	G	E	L	E	M	E	N	T	O
G	A	S	P	N	M	N	Q	J	V	M	H	D	N	U	W	V	C	E	C	X	R	Y

1. The difference between the Dew Point and the Bubble Point.
2. The form of matter that is an easily compressible fluid
3. A mixture of at least two different liquids.
4. That time period of a refrigeration cycle when the system is not operating.
5. In some air conditioning systems, vacuum is used to operate dampers and controls in system.
6. Special high efficiency device (pump) used create deep vacuum within an AC
7. Any products that are fully manufactured, charged, and hermetically sealed in a factory with five pounds or less of refrigerant
8. A separation process in which a certain quantity of a mixture is divided during a phase transition
9. Single use cylinders. Empty cylinders should have the pressure reduced to zero and the cylinder rendered unusable.
10. Light provided with test leads, used to test or probe electrical circuits to determine if they are alive.
11. The temperature where a refrigerant exists in both liquid and vapor form relative to its measured pressure.
12. The atom found in CFC and HCFC refrigerants that destroys ozone in the stratosphere.
13. The process of cooling or chilling.
14. Temperature at which molecular motion ceases.
15. The process in which a gas flows through a small hole in a container.
16. Electrical resistance mounted in or around liquid receiver, used to maintain head pressures when ambient temperature is at freezing or below freezing.
17. An instrument for measuring resistance in ohms.
18. A form of testing for high pressure cylinders.

A. Temperature Glide
D. Refrigeration
G. Effusion
J. Absolute Zero Temperature
M. Hydrostatic
P. Small appliance

B. Ohmmeter
E. Vacuum Control System
H. Disposable cylinders
K. Chlorine
N. Off Cycle
Q. Saturation Temperature

C. Gas
F. Fractionation
I. Test Light
L. Azeotroph
O. Vacuum Pump
R. Receiver Heating Element

N. Find the hidden words. The words have been placed horizontally, vertically, or diagonally. When you locate a word, draw an ellipse around it.

E	V	A	P	O	R	A	T	O	R	C	O	I	L	P	I	S	T	O	N	H	P	V
W	W	V	D	G	V	Q	J	V	K	L	F	I	G	H	A	B	D	J	E	G	M	Y
T	G	I	Y	F	J	Y	T	R	Y	B	G	S	A	A	S	P	Q	U	H	V	F	P
C	Q	Q	T	R	K	K	Q	W	D	A	B	O	U	L	N	R	V	N	Y	Q	B	Q
O	O	W	Y	W	W	W	S	X	I	F	A	L	E	O	L	O	L	C	D	K	I	Y
N	R	V	A	P	O	R	V	H	Z	P	C	A	Y	N	E	O	O	T	R	N	V	B
D	A	D	S	O	R	P	T	I	O	N	K	T	T	X	A	L	J	I	O	L	J	A
E	Q	Z	C	Y	H	S	T	T	B	U	P	E	B	F	K	L	H	O	C	S	Q	C
N	M	O	A	Z	I	C	B	Q	I	J	R	J	B	D	R	U	L	N	A	Y	T	K
S	L	A	T	E	N	T	H	E	A	T	E	V	Y	L	A	I	J	B	R	R	Y	S
E	C	O	X	U	W	I	D	F	D	D	S	K	X	J	T	M	B	O	B	N	Y	E
R	T	H	E	R	M	O	S	T	A	T	S	M	P	X	E	I	S	X	O	Q	G	A
C	I	H	E	A	D	P	R	E	S	S	U	R	E	C	L	Q	J	G	N	H	C	T
O	W	B	W	U	E	G	T	Z	G	E	R	S	U	P	E	R	H	E	A	T	Y	I
I	A	K	O	P	R	E	F	R	I	G	E	R	A	T	I	O	N	H	T	K	N	N
L	V	U	U	Q	K	Y	Q	M	T	W	V	A	C	U	U	M	G	A	U	G	E	G

1. cause to be or remain alone or apart from others.
2. A chemical used in fire extinguishing.
3. Close fitting part which moves up and down in a cylinder.
4. The adhesion of a thin layer of molecules of a gas or liquid to a solid object.
5. Dissipates heat from the refrigerant.
6. Pressure in low side of refrigerating system; also called suction pressure or low side pressure.
7. Heat energy absorbed in process of changing form of substance without change in temperature or pressure.
8. A temperature control device. Typically mounted in conditioned space.
9. The temperature rise within an evaporator or suction line assembly from the evaporator's saturation temperature.
10. The process of cooling or chilling.
11. Group of electrical terminals housed in protective box or container.
12. Pressure which exists in condensing side of refrigerating system.
13. The Gaseous state of any kind of matter that normally exists as a liquid or solid.
14. The rate at which an appliance is losing refrigerant.
15. Where heat is absorbed by warm air passing across. Liquid refrigerant boils as it is metered into coil, and changes from liquid to vapor.
16. A compound containing only the elements hydrogen and carbon.
17. Instrument used to measure pressures below atmospheric pressure.
18. Fluid opening

A. Head Pressure	B. Super Heat	C. Vacuum Gauge	D. Evaporator Coil	E. Piston
F. Back Seating	G. Adsorption	H. Thermostat	I. Condenser Coil	J. Vapor
K. Leak Rate	L. Refrigeration	M. Junction Box	N. Hydrocarbon	O. Latent Heat
P. Back Pressure	Q. Isolate	R. Halon		

O. Find the hidden words. The words have been placed horizontally, vertically, or diagonally. When you locate a word, draw an ellipse around it.

M	V	W	V	I	A	H	P	F	R	A	C	T	I	O	N	A	T	I	O	N	H	M
A	B	S	O	L	U	T	E	Z	E	R	O	T	E	M	P	E	R	A	T	U	R	E
J	S	S	P	F	I	E	L	D	P	O	L	E	R	E	T	P	W	U	N	E	W	T
Z	T	M	I	C	L	M	W	E	V	A	P	O	R	A	T	O	R	C	O	I	L	E
N	T	Z	D	T	I	B	F	B	N	I	R	M	B	U	C	E	C	M	Q	I	T	R
R	A	C	T	I	V	E	R	E	C	O	V	E	R	Y	G	S	Q	W	D	I	Z	I
Y	V	C	K	V	Y	V	E	L	O	C	I	T	Y	H	E	A	D	S	M	X	V	N
R	K	U	R	E	F	R	I	G	E	R	A	N	T	C	I	R	C	U	I	T	G	G
E	M	J	Y	D	A	M	P	E	R	Y	J	D	D	Z	Z	W	N	T	C	T	L	D
I	N	S	U	L	A	T	I	O	N	D	M	U	Y	W	C	P	M	P	C	F	W	E
J	S	C	O	M	P	R	E	S	S	O	R	C	F	Q	Y	Y	Z	L	C	F	G	V
X	F	Z	V	Y	W	G	W	B	W	Z	B	T	K	I	N	G	V	A	L	V	E	I
P	I	N	C	H	O	F	F	T	O	O	L	W	U	J	T	N	S	Q	R	X	H	C
S	B	Z	A	C	C	U	M	U	L	A	T	O	R	L	U	I	X	P	U	Q	R	E
F	W	O	T	X	G	Q	Q	J	R	E	F	R	I	G	E	R	A	N	T	F	E	A
K	Q	T	E	C	H	N	I	C	I	A	N	K	M	A	N	O	M	E	T	E	R	K

1. The parts of an appliance that are normally connected to each other and are designed to contain refrigerant.
2. The fluid used for heat transfer in a refrigeration system, which absorbs heat during evaporation at low temperature and pressure, and releases heat during condensation.
3. In flowing fluid, height of fluid equivalent to its velocity pressure.
4. Round or rectangular pipes or controlled paths acting as conduit for return, mixed, makeup, supply or exhaust air.
5. Temperature at which molecular motion ceases.
6. Where heat is absorbed by warm air passing across. Liquid refrigerant boils as it is metered into coil, and changes from liquid to vapor.
7. A combination shut-off and service value typically used on the inlet and outlet of a compressor.
8. Any material or substance which has the ability to retard the flow or transfer of heat.
9. Part of stator of motor which concentrates magnetic field of field winding.
10. Any person who performs maintenance, service, or repair that could reasonably be expected to release class I or class II substances into the atmosphere.
11. Valve for controlling airflow. Found in duct work, movable plate opens and closes to control airflow.
12. Storage tank which receives liquid refrigerant from evaporator and prevents it from flowing into suction line.
13. Instrument to measuring pressure of gases and vapors.
14. Equipment that has its own compressor or pump.
15. Creates pressure drop to allow liquid refrigerant to boil and absorb latent heat.
16. Device used to press walls of a tubing together until fluid flow ceases.
17. The heart or "pump" within an air conditioning or heat pump system.
18. A separation process in which a certain quantity of a mixture is divided during a phase transition

A. Pinch off Tool
D. Absolute Zero Temperature
G. Field Pole
J. Metering Device
M. Evaporator Coil
P. Refrigerant circuit

B. Velocity Head
E. Compressor
H. Ductwork
K. Technician
N. Refrigerant
Q. King Valve

C. Accumulator
F. Fractionation
I. Damper
L. Manometer
O. Insulation
R. Active recovery

A. Find the hidden words. The words have been placed horizontally, vertically, or diagonally. When you locate a word, draw an ellipse around it.

I	G	A	C	T	I	V	E	R	E	C	O	V	E	R	Y	L	G	H	I	F	E	O
S	X	B	J	B	I	O	U	P	W	Z	L	O	W	P	R	E	S	S	U	R	E	S
N	V	D	O	H	N	L	Y	X	A	R	I	V	B	V	L	R	F	M	H	T	A	E
Q	I	A	U	J	G	W	B	J	X	X	B	A	D	S	O	R	P	T	I	O	N	D
I	T	R	L	I	E	Z	Y	P	U	R	G	E	U	N	I	T	V	J	L	O	W	T
R	C	Q	E	J	C	C	M	V	Y	N	X	M	C	Y	G	O	W	N	T	G	R	T
B	U	J	B	N	J	Y	R	T	C	V	O	L	T	T	H	E	R	M	M	H	R	E
H	G	S	G	V	O	H	T	E	S	T	L	I	G	H	T	I	S	O	L	A	T	E
A	J	F	T	W	C	A	L	A	T	E	N	T	H	E	A	T	R	H	M	X	U	P
L	C	Y	A	V	A	E	C	O	N	I	M	I	Z	E	R	B	O	D	X	H	U	U
O	D	I	S	P	O	S	A	B	L	E	C	Y	L	I	N	D	E	R	S	Z	V	G
N	C	H	E	H	Y	S	J	S	E	R	V	I	C	E	M	A	N	I	F	O	L	D
J	W	A	M	Z	N	R	R	M	I	C	R	O	N	E	V	H	X	F	T	D	L	R
E	G	K	K	C	K	Z	D	I	S	T	I	L	L	A	T	I	O	N	W	G	T	P
A	B	S	O	L	U	T	E	H	U	M	I	D	I	T	Y	Z	I	Q	W	W	S	O
D	U	N	C	B	M	A	C	R	T	U	B	I	N	G	P	A	R	A	L	L	E	L

1. Heat energy absorbed in process of changing form of substance without change in temperature or pressure.
2. Quantity of heat equivalent to 100,000 Btu.
3. Change in temperature of a gas on expansion through a porous plug from a high pressure to a lower pressure.
4. The action of purifying a liquid by a process of heating and cooling.
5. One thousandth of a millimeter.
6. An independent refrigeration system that separates the non-condensables from the refrigerant and re-condenses and collects any refrigerant in the exhaust vent stream.
7. Electrical "pressure" applied to a circuit.
8. A refrigerant has a boiling point above 10C or 50F at atmospheric pressure.
9. Light provided with test leads, used to test or probe electrical circuits to determine if they are alive.
10. Tubing used in refrigeration which has ends to keep tubing clean and dry.
11. A device equipped with gauges and manual valves, used by serviceman to service refrigerating systems.
12. Equipment that has its own compressor or pump.
13. Amount of moisture in the air, indicated in grains per cubic foot.
14. cause to be or remain alone or apart from others.
15. A mechanism that removes flash gas from the evaporator.
16. Undesirable component in many refrigeration lubricants, which may separate out of solution if cooled sufficiently.
17. Side by side and having the same distance continuously between them.
18. Single use cylinders. Empty cylinders should have the pressure reduced to zero and the cylinder rendered unusable.
19. The adhesion of a thin layer of molecules of a gas or liquid to a solid object.
20. A chemical used in fire extinguishing.

A. Latent Heat	B. Volt
E. Parallel	F. Test Light
I. Halon	J. Isolate
M. Joule	N. Purge unit
Q. Therm	R. Active recovery

C. Wax	D. Adsorption
G. Absolute Humidity	H. Micron
K. ACR Tubing	L. Econimizer
O. Low pressure	P. Service Manifold
S. Distillation	T. Disposable cylinders

125

B. Find the hidden words. The words have been placed horizontally, vertically, or diagonally. When you locate a word, draw an ellipse around it.

P	H	E	A	T	E	X	C	H	A	N	G	E	R	E	D	Y	R	D	S	R	K	R
A	B	S	O	L	U	T	E	Z	E	R	O	T	E	M	P	E	R	A	T	U	R	E
I	I	J	S	U	B	C	O	O	L	I	N	G	D	M	Q	E	I	W	O	C	M	Z
J	S	U	P	E	R	H	E	A	T	D	N	K	O	S	E	K	P	F	R	D	M	R
P	H	A	L	I	D	E	R	E	F	R	I	G	E	R	A	N	T	S	A	Q	G	D
O	M	I	S	O	L	A	T	E	C	D	S	L	C	F	H	E	A	T	G	T	A	B
R	E	C	E	I	V	E	R	H	E	A	T	I	N	G	E	L	E	M	E	N	T	B
Y	V	F	N	R	J	G	A	P	R	E	C	E	I	V	E	R	O	C	C	L	M	A
B	A	C	F	X	M	X	Z	X	F	H	P	R	E	S	S	U	R	E	Y	Q	J	V
Q	C	S	K	E	A	C	T	I	V	E	R	E	C	O	V	E	R	Y	L	U	S	D
I	U	R	A	P	M	U	I	J	R	E	F	R	I	G	E	R	A	T	I	O	N	Q
Q	U	O	M	B	P	O	H	M	Q	D	Q	J	X	I	H	C	B	E	N	S	X	X
I	W	N	P	I	E	F	J	P	S	C	M	O	T	O	R	I	T	J	D	R	B	K
B	P	D	D	O	R	J	D	I	S	T	I	L	L	A	T	I	O	N	E	G	L	Q
B	A	C	K	S	E	A	T	I	N	G	V	O	T	S	A	I	M	W	R	M	U	P
B	E	Y	D	S	C	A	L	I	B	R	A	T	E	M	V	T	H	L	S	E	E	D

1. Process whereas additional sensible heat (as opposed to latent heat) is removed from condensed refrigerant liquid prior to the metering device.
2. Invisible energy caused by the motion of molecules within any substance or matter.
3. cause to be or remain alone or apart from others.
4. The action of purifying a liquid by a process of heating and cooling.
5. Unit of measure referring to the flow of electrons within a circuit.
6. Larger cylinders used for storing refrigerant to be transferred to smaller refillable cylinders.
7. Electrical resistance mounted in or around liquid receiver, used to maintain head pressures when ambient temperature is at freezing or below freezing.
8. A standard unit of measure for electrical resistance.
9. High-efficiency design motor used on virtually all of today's HVAC & R equipment requiring motors.
10. Equipment that has its own compressor or pump.
11. The temperature rise within an evaporator or suction line assembly from the evaporator's saturation temperature.
12. Receives high pressure liquid from the condenser
13. Fluid opening
14. To determine; position indicators as required to obtain accurate measurements.
15. Temperature at which molecular motion ceases.
16. The force exerted per unit area of surface.
17. The process of cooling or chilling.
18. Reduction in pressure below atmospheric pressure.
19. A device for the transfer of heat energy from the source to the conveying medium, with the latter often being air or water.
20. Family of refrigerants containing halogen chemicals.
21. Low pressure

A. Blue
D. Ampere
G. Back Seating
J. Vacuum
M. Refrigeration
P. Receiver
S. Sub Cooling

B. Isolate
E. OHM
H. Heat
K. PSC Motor
N. Absolute Zero Temperature
Q. Distillation
T. Receiver Heating Element

C. Super Heat
F. Active recovery
I. Halide Refrigerants
L. Pressure
O. Storage cylinders
R. Heat Exchanger
U. Calibrate

C. Find the hidden words. The words have been placed horizontally, vertically, or diagonally. When you locate a word, draw an ellipse around it.

H	B	L	U	E	T	S	X	L	M	A	N	O	M	E	T	E	R	V	B	H	N	M
Z	L	S	A	G	C	U	G	K	L	R	O	I	N	P	C	S	V	U	O	T	Q	E
G	D	I	J	Z	U	P	T	U	T	E	C	H	N	I	C	I	A	N	R	D	H	V
P	A	S	S	I	V	E	R	E	C	O	V	E	R	Y	N	N	X	A	I	I	U	W
R	E	C	O	V	E	R	Y	B	D	F	W	N	O	S	V	Q	U	E	F	V	M	T
Z	G	N	W	I	S	H	H	K	Q	H	I	N	P	H	V	A	U	P	I	Q	I	O
T	V	U	Q	N	U	E	R	R	K	N	S	E	Q	X	B	D	P	S	C	Z	D	Q
O	P	A	R	T	I	A	L	P	R	E	S	S	U	R	E	I	A	C	E	M	I	K
W	X	I	Y	H	X	T	U	D	E	H	Y	D	R	A	T	E	V	M	P	E	T	P
R	E	C	Y	C	L	E	T	E	S	T	L	I	G	H	T	B	X	O	L	F	Y	Q
A	A	B	S	O	R	B	E	N	T	C	R	C	A	P	A	C	I	T	A	N	C	E
A	X	X	Y	D	R	P	N	D	G	B	E	B	F	S	J	J	U	O	T	Q	L	S
C	O	M	P	O	U	N	D	G	A	U	G	E	K	N	S	W	Z	R	E	A	W	D
Y	Y	Z	O	A	C	T	I	V	A	T	E	D	A	L	U	M	I	N	A	X	I	D
P	M	T	F	A	B	S	O	L	U	T	E	T	E	M	P	E	R	A	T	U	R	E
T	A	B	S	O	R	P	T	I	O	N	R	E	F	R	I	G	E	R	A	T	O	R

1. Requires the assistance of components such as the appliance or unit's compressor to remove the refrigerant from the appliance.
2. Property of non-conductor that permits storage of electrical energy in an electrostatic field.
3. To remove water from a system.
4. A passive throttling device, comprised of a small opening, located upstream of the evaporator.
5. The Pressure exerted by a particular Gas in a mixture.
6. Light provided with test leads, used to test or probe electrical circuits to determine if they are alive.
7. The temperature rise within an evaporator or suction line assembly from the evaporator's saturation temperature.
8. Instrument to measuring pressure of gases and vapors.
9. Any person who performs maintenance, service, or repair that could reasonably be expected to release class I or class II substances into the atmosphere.

10. Refrigerator which creates low temperatures by using the cooling effect formed when a refrigerant is absorbed by chemical substance.
11. The process of collecting used refrigerant.
12. Low pressure
13. The total amount of moisture in air.
14. Chemical used as a drier or desiccant.
15. High-efficiency design motor used on virtually all of today's HVAC & R equipment requiring motors.
16. Substance with ability to take up, or absorb another substance.
17. To extract refrigerant from an appliance and clean refrigerant for reuse without meeting all of the requirements for reclamation.
18. A temperature scale in which the lowest temperature that can be attained theoretically is zero
19. Measures low pressure and vacuum.

A. Absolute Temperature	B. Absorption Refrigerator	C. Blue	D. Recycle
E. Orifice Plate	F. Activated Alumina	G. Manometer	H. Capacitance
I. Super Heat	J. Technician	K. Dehydrate	L. Passive recovery
M. PSC Motor	N. Absorbent	O. Compound gauge	P. Recovery
Q. Humidity	R. Test Light	S. Partial Pressure	

D. Find the hidden words. The words have been placed horizontally, vertically, or diagonally. When you locate a word, draw an ellipse around it.

```
W  T  K  N  Y  F  V  E  R  Y  H  I  G  H  P  R  E  S  S  U  R  E  A
R  M  K  C  U  A  R  B  B  O  V  C  G  N  N  L  Z  D  K  I  U  S  X
E  C  B  K  N  H  X  V  G  A  Q  I  G  I  L  Y  A  O  S  F  X  F  H
F  O  U  N  Q  H  A  L  I  D  E  R  E  F  R  I  G  E  R  A  N  T  S
R  H  B  B  N  Y  S  L  U  G  D  P  K  I  O  H  S  G  T  O  H  M  T
I  M  B  C  G  V  U  N  F  E  V  A  P  O  R  A  T  O  R  C  O  I  L
G  M  L  H  V  U  P  A  E  N  I  T  R  O  G  E  N  B  N  Y  P  S  C
E  E  E  L  A  X  E  M  A  C  T  I  V  E  R  E  C  O  V  E  R  Y  Q
R  T  P  O  P  O  R  U  M  T  Z  J  M  T  N  S  V  A  W  Q  I  H  Y
A  E  O  R  O  L  H  R  K  F  I  E  L  D  P  O  L  E  T  I  V  B  I
T  R  I  I  R  W  E  X  V  R  K  M  N  V  Y  S  Y  U  Z  T  W  I  U
I  S  N  N  B  F  A  E  F  W  Q  D  E  M  I  N  I  M  U  S  I  T  R
O  F  T  E  C  W  T  G  Y  S  A  F  E  T  Y  C  O  N  T  R  O  L  L
N  L  A  M  P  E  R  E  D  M  R  B  C  F  H  E  Y  X  K  M  Y  R  U
B  D  E  H  Y  D  R  A  T  E  Z  Q  U  W  D  R  B  E  J  Q  V  H  S
C  M  Z  J  O  Q  S  T  A  T  I  C  H  E  A  D  K  R  S  Q  V  X  A
```

1. Equipment that has its own compressor or pump.
2. Unit of measure referring to the flow of electrons within a circuit.
3. The temperature rise within an evaporator or suction line assembly from the evaporator's saturation temperature.
4. To remove water from a system.
5. Where heat is absorbed by warm air passing across. Liquid refrigerant boils as it is metered into coil, and changes from liquid to vapor.
6. An instrument for measuring resistance in ohms.
7. A refrigerant has a boiling point below minus 50C or minus 58F at atmospheric pressure.
8. The Gaseous state of any kind of matter that normally exists as a liquid or solid.
9. The atom found in CFC and HCFC refrigerants that destroys ozone in the stratosphere.
10. The moving of heat from an undesirable location, to that of a location where its presence is less undesirable.
11. Device used to electrically shut down a refrigerating unit when unsafe pressures and
12. Latin for the least amount of Refrigerant you can release into the atmosphere.
13. The temperature at which the non-azeotropic blend first begins to evaporate.
14. Family of refrigerants containing halogen chemicals.
15. Gas used for leak detection.
16. Part of stator of motor which concentrates magnetic field of field winding.
17. A standard unit of measure for electrical resistance.
18. Pressure of fluid expressed in terms of height of column of the fluid, such as water or mercury.

A. Evaporator Coil
E. Bubble Point
I. Safety Control
M. OHM
Q. Dehydrate

B. Very high pressure
F. Chlorine
J. Nitrogen
N. Super Heat
R. Vapor

C. De Minimus
G. Halide Refrigerants
K. Static Head
O. Ohmmeter

D. Active recovery
H. Refrigeration
L. Ampere
P. Field Pole

E. Find the hidden words. The words have been placed horizontally, vertically, or diagonally. When you locate a word, draw an ellipse around it.

B	U	N	C	T	H	E	R	M	L	D	D	J	Q	M	I	B	Y	V	J	D	N	V
R	G	E	O	V	G	H	O	N	Y	D	E	H	Y	D	R	A	T	E	K	Y	A	O
E	A	U	N	D	T	B	E	X	P	A	N	S	I	O	N	D	E	V	I	C	E	Q
C	U	T	D	L	Z	J	Y	T	T	A	B	J	X	F	K	I	S	T	E	N	R	N
O	G	R	E	A	Q	V	K	S	A	F	E	T	Y	C	O	N	T	R	O	L	V	P
V	E	A	N	B	C	J	M	D	P	G	W	L	S	Q	Z	L	A	K	K	A	T	A
E	M	L	S	H	I	G	H	P	R	E	S	S	U	R	E	V	T	U	W	T	J	C
R	A	I	E	A	B	S	O	L	U	T	E	H	U	M	I	D	I	T	Y	M	I	C
Y	N	Z	R	M	I	C	R	O	N	R	E	C	L	A	I	M	C	C	Q	O	R	U
T	I	E	M	S	U	B	C	O	O	L	I	N	G	W	Q	T	H	K	V	S	A	M
D	F	R	T	P	I	S	T	O	N	X	R	K	N	X	T	R	E	I	Z	P	Q	U
M	O	N	T	R	E	A	L	P	R	O	T	O	C	O	L	C	A	F	B	H	H	L
D	L	G	V	A	N	M	G	Y	M	R	T	Q	T	P	C	A	D	W	P	E	V	A
R	D	B	R	I	T	I	S	H	T	H	E	R	M	A	L	U	N	I	T	R	N	T
T	I	I	W	D	N	I	T	R	O	G	E	N	R	Z	D	Z	P	N	L	E	O	O
M	N	H	A	L	I	D	E	R	E	F	R	I	G	E	R	A	N	T	S	P	U	R

1. Treaty among nations designed to protect the stratospheric ozone layer.
2. A unit of Pressure equal to exactly 760 mmHg
3. Close fitting part which moves up and down in a cylinder.
4. Condenses high pressure gas from the compressor to high pressure liquid.
5. One thousandth of a millimeter.
6. Pressure of fluid expressed in terms of height of column of the fluid, such as water or mercury.
7. Substance used to counteract acids, in refrigeration system.
8. Quantity of heat equivalent to 100,000 Btu.
9. Amount of moisture in the air, indicated in grains per cubic foot.
10. A refrigerant has a boiling point between minus 50C and 10C degrees at atmospheric pressure.
11. Device used to electrically shut down a refrigerating unit when unsafe pressures and

12. A tool that measures pressure readings at different points in the refrigeration system.
13. Converting recycled refrigerant into a product to be reused.
14. Gas used for leak detection.
15. Family of refrigerants containing halogen chemicals.
16. To remove water from a system.
17. Represents the amount of energy required to raise one pound of water one degree Fahrenheit.
18. Converts high pressure liquid to low pressure vapor
19. The process of collecting used refrigerant.
20. Accumulates any low pressure liquid from the evaporator so it can vaporize before entering the compressor
21. Process whereas additional sensible heat (as opposed to latent heat) is removed from condensed refrigerant liquid prior to the metering device.

A. Reclaim
E. Halide Refrigerants
I. Gauge manifold
M. Dehydrate
Q. High pressure
U. Piston

B. Accumulator
F. Neutralizer
J. Safety Control
N. Expansion device
R. Therm

C. Micron
G. Recovery
K. Static Head
O. Sub Cooling
S. British Thermal Unit

D. Nitrogen
H. Absolute Humidity
L. Condenser
P. Atmosphere
T. Montreal Protocol

F. Find the hidden words. The words have been placed horizontally, vertically, or diagonally. When you locate a word, draw an ellipse around it.

```
W  G  N  L  K  O  A  R  T  J  D  C  E  V  A  P  O  R  A  T  O  R  D
X  B  Z  O  F  H  Y  D  R  O  S  T  A  T  I  C  N  W  V  G  P  W  X
H  I  G  H  P  R  E  S  S  U  R  E  O  D  J  X  T  B  U  S  X  W  F
O  Z  O  N  E  L  A  Y  E  R  R  E  F  R  I  G  E  R  A  N  T  X  U
A  B  S  O  L  U  T  E  T  E  M  P  E  R  A  T  U  R  E  D  P  T  P
U  L  T  R  A  V  I  O  L  E  T  R  A  D  I  A  T  I  O  N  T  U  M
I  D  W  G  J  F  Y  R  Y  O  D  D  P  R  Q  O  V  K  R  T  E  Z  H
J  J  F  A  W  C  T  C  X  C  G  E  M  D  C  O  L  D  O  T  M  S  X
R  E  F  R  I  G  E  R  A  N  T  C  I  R  C  U  I  T  Z  S  P  V  K
W  S  T  O  R  A  G  E  C  Y  L  I  N  D  E  R  S  E  T  H  E  O  G
S  A  D  D  L  E  V  A  L  V  E  B  G  H  E  C  V  U  E  Z  R  U  Q
D  E  W  P  O  I  N  T  F  N  C  E  F  O  D  E  H  Y  D  R  A  T  E
A  C  E  N  T  E  R  P  O  R  T  U  L  W  C  O  C  U  D  N  T  R  B
E  X  M  F  M  T  H  V  H  Y  D  R  O  C  A  R  B  O  N  M  U  V  S
A  K  A  C  T  I  V  A  T  E  D  C  A  R  B  O  N  S  Y  O  R  Z  B
V  A  P  O  R  P  A  R  T  I  A  L  P  R  E  S  S  U  R  E  E  S  L
```

1. Unit used for measuring relative loudness of sounds.
2. Degree of hotness or coldness as measured by a thermometer
3. The temperature at which the non-azeotropic blend first begins to condense.
4. Breaks down the CFCs and frees the chlorine ion at stratosphere.
5. A form of testing for high pressure cylinders.
6. Specially processed carbon used as a filter drier; commonly used to clean air.
7. A refrigerant has a boiling point between minus 50C and 10C degrees at atmospheric pressure.
8. To remove water from a system.
9. The Gaseous state of any kind of matter that normally exists as a liquid or solid.
10. The Pressure exerted by a particular Gas in a mixture.
11. A substance produces a refrigerating or cooling effect while expanding or vaporizing.
12. The parts of an appliance that are normally connected to each other and are designed to contain refrigerant.
13. Larger cylinders used for storing refrigerant to be transferred to smaller refillable cylinders.
14. Protective shield for Earth from the sun's harmful ultraviolet (UV) rays in the stratosphere layer that extends about 6 to 30 miles above earth.
15. Temperature measured from absolute zero.
16. Connects manifold to recovery device.
17. Self piercing valve body designed to be permanently silver brazed or clamped to refrigerant tubing surface.
18. A sensation felt as a result of the absence of heat.
19. Evaporates low pressure vapor from the expansion device
20. A compound containing only the elements hydrogen and carbon.

A. Cold	B. Ozone layer	C. Refrigerant	D. Evaporator
E. High pressure	F. Saddle Valve	G. Decibel	H. Ultraviolet Radiation
I. Dew Point	J. Dehydrate	K. Vapor	L. Refrigerant circuit
M. Hydrostatic	N. Temperature	O. Hydrocarbon	P. Absolute Temperature
Q. Activated Carbon	R. Center port	S. Partial Pressure	T. Storage cylinders

G. Find the hidden words. The words have been placed horizontally, vertically, or diagonally. When you locate a word, draw an ellipse around it.

L	M	O	D	I	S	P	O	S	A	B	L	E	C	Y	L	I	N	D	E	R	S	L
B	U	H	X	M	P	E	I	O	C	A	L	C	I	U	M	S	U	L	F	A	T	E
C	G	I	Q	F	P	I	O	E	J	Q	L	Y	F	G	K	S	Z	Q	A	E	Y	M
A	J	B	R	M	F	W	M	P	R	C	S	C	O	M	P	R	E	S	S	O	R	S
P	U	E	S	M	A	L	L	A	P	P	L	I	A	N	C	E	Z	G	Z	O	G	F
A	N	D	E	C	I	B	E	L	P	Q	B	V	D	M	V	N	X	E	M	Y	E	D
C	C	Q	U	H	Y	S	K	M	T	E	C	H	N	I	C	I	A	N	C	C	O	S
I	T	O	S	F	A	T	M	O	S	P	H	E	R	E	B	H	D	S	L	O	J	U
T	I	D	E	N	S	I	T	Y	P	A	S	C	A	L	S	L	A	W	P	M	H	K
A	O	A	B	S	O	L	U	T	E	P	R	E	S	S	U	R	E	F	O	P	Z	K
N	N	I	P	L	F	D	O	P	O	F	Z	B	V	W	M	F	S	N	B	O	J	G
C	B	K	G	T	G	T	M	B	O	J	O	I	J	B	I	A	K	S	Z	U	E	M
E	O	S	A	F	E	T	Y	C	O	N	T	R	O	L	C	R	D	M	L	N	E	Q
N	X	C	P	R	E	S	S	U	R	E	D	R	P	M	R	A	C	B	G	D	B	Y
D	S	M	I	S	C	I	B	L	E	Q	B	V	Y	D	O	D	O	E	A	F	V	Y
Q	D	W	O	A	Y	W	V	G	Q	G	D	Q	V	M	N	B	H	M	C	H	C	H

1. Group of electrical terminals housed in protective box or container.
2. Any products that are fully manufactured, charged, and hermetically sealed in a factory with five pounds or less of refrigerant
3. Any person who performs maintenance, service, or repair that could reasonably be expected to release class I or class II substances into the atmosphere.
4. Device used to electrically shut down a refrigerating unit when unsafe pressures and
5. Property of non-conductor that permits storage of electrical energy in an electrostatic field.
6. A substance formed by a union of two or more elements
7. Gauge pressure plus atmospheric pressure (14.7 lbs. per sq. in.).
8. One thousandth of a millimeter.
9. Unit used for measuring relative loudness of sounds.
10. The force exerted per unit area of surface.
11. A pressure imposed upon a fluid is transmitted equally in all directions.
12. The heart or "pump" within an air conditioning or heat pump system.
13. The mass per unit volume of a substance or solution.
14. Single use cylinders. Empty cylinders should have the pressure reduced to zero and the cylinder rendered unusable.
15. Forming a homogeneous mixture of liquids when added together.
16. Chemical compound which is used as a drying agent or desiccant in liquid line filter dryers.
17. Unit of electrical capacity; capacity of a condenser which, when charged with one coulomb of electricity, gives difference of potential of one volt.
18. A unit of Pressure equal to exactly 760 mmHg

A. Miscible	B. Decibel	C. Farad	D. Junction Box
E. Compressor	F. Calcium Sulfate	G. Pascals Law	H. Disposable cylinders
I. Atmosphere	J. Micron	K. Density	L. Pressure
M. Small appliance	N. Capacitance	O. Absolute Pressure	P. Technician
Q. Safety Control	R. Compound		

131

H. Find the hidden words. The words have been placed horizontally, vertically, or diagonally. When you locate a word, draw an ellipse around it.

Z	J	C	Q	F	J	W	Z	P	S	Y	C	H	R	O	M	E	T	E	R	Q	H	G
E	A	L	C	O	L	D	Q	N	B	I	F	D	X	C	K	Y	F	D	R	N	X	N
D	O	V	J	D	N	M	K	S	N	Z	G	Z	Z	W	L	U	A	L	U	L	H	U
B	A	Z	J	X	Z	E	C	A	L	O	R	I	M	E	T	E	R	L	B	R	A	J
C	D	C	D	A	S	J	L	E	A	K	D	E	T	E	C	T	O	R	Q	I	L	C
A	S	R	P	C	A	S	O	O	F	F	C	Y	C	L	E	D	Q	C	K	B	I	T
J	O	R	B	C	T	C	H	B	U	B	B	L	E	P	O	I	N	T	C	J	D	M
W	R	Z	G	U	M	O	M	I	Y	R	C	O	M	P	R	E	S	S	O	R	E	V
Q	B	D	X	M	O	V	M	E	A	Z	E	O	T	R	O	P	H	C	D	R	T	J
T	E	U	F	U	S	J	E	V	T	U	O	R	E	C	O	V	E	R	Y	D	O	R
S	N	A	H	L	P	Z	T	P	A	R	T	I	A	L	P	R	E	S	S	U	R	E
A	T	U	G	A	H	M	E	R	C	O	S	S	X	W	N	M	F	P	W	R	C	F
Z	S	J	H	T	E	E	R	D	C	H	A	R	L	E	S	L	A	W	B	G	H	L
Z	F	H	Z	O	R	V	I	E	X	B	Y	Q	M	P	U	A	C	H	M	H	G	P
Y	G	Z	M	R	E	A	E	X	P	A	N	S	I	O	N	D	E	V	I	C	E	P
Q	S	A	B	S	O	L	U	T	E	T	E	M	P	E	R	A	T	U	R	E	Q	C

1. An instrument for measuring resistance in ohms.
2. Type of torch used to detect halogen refrigerant leaks.
3. A unit of Pressure equal to exactly 760 mmHg
4. The temperature at which the non-azeotropic blend first begins to evaporate.
5. The Pressure exerted by a particular Gas in a mixture.
6. Device used to measure quantities of heat or determine specific heats.
7. Device or instrument such as a halide torch, an electronic sniffer; or soap solution used to detect leaks.
8. A mixture of at least two different liquids.
9. Either a sling type, or electronic. Instrument used to determine wet bulb temperatures and relative humidity.
10. A sensation felt as a result of the absence of heat.
11. The process of collecting used refrigerant.
12. States that the volume occupied by a gas at a constant Pressure is directly proportional to the absolute temperature.
13. Converts high pressure liquid to low pressure vapor
14. Substance which has property to hold molecules of fluids without causing a chemical or physical change.
15. The heart or "pump" within an air conditioning or heat pump system.
16. Temperature measured from absolute zero.
17. Accumulates any low pressure liquid from the evaporator so it can vaporize before entering the compressor
18. That time period of a refrigeration cycle when the system is not operating.

A. Azeotroph	B. Halide Torch	C. Accumulator	D. Bubble Point
E. Leak Detector	F. Cold	G. Psychrometer	H. Off Cycle
I. Ohmmeter	J. Absolute Temperature	K. Recovery	L. Partial Pressure
M. Atmosphere	N. Compressor	O. Expansion device	P. Adsorbent
Q. Charles Law	R. Calorimeter		

I. Find the hidden words. The words have been placed horizontally, vertically, or diagonally. When you locate a word, draw an ellipse around it.

L	L	R	G	A	U	G	E	M	A	N	I	F	O	L	D	D	E	C	I	B	E	L
Q	O	E	N	K	R	Y	A	C	H	A	R	L	E	S	L	A	W	F	I	I	O	Y
B	T	F	J	X	E	V	I	F	W	Q	T	Z	W	B	Y	H	M	V	S	N	E	K
V	E	R	B	Y	C	A	C	O	M	P	R	E	S	S	O	R	G	N	R	I	L	B
X	G	I	K	H	Y	P	P	S	Y	C	H	R	O	M	E	T	E	R	Y	T	Q	R
H	M	G	T	M	C	O	S	L	U	N	O	A	C	R	T	U	B	I	N	G	C	M
F	M	E	V	D	L	R	D	D	W	S	K	R	E	V	A	C	U	A	T	I	O	N
V	O	R	N	E	E	R	T	E	M	P	E	R	A	T	U	R	E	G	L	I	D	E
C	P	A	Q	R	J	S	E	A	F	R	R	I	M	Q	E	S	Y	O	W	A	G	M
P	C	T	D	G	D	B	B	G	A	M	Y	F	H	A	I	F	W	X	T	M	T	I
O	R	I	F	I	C	E	P	L	A	T	E	B	M	P	B	L	U	E	L	P	M	S
U	K	O	C	G	Y	W	Z	R	Y	C	Z	L	J	N	H	Q	Y	A	T	E	T	C
L	B	N	L	H	Z	W	P	A	R	A	L	L	E	L	B	U	C	E	C	R	N	I
R	U	I	R	Z	Z	C	P	Y	O	J	Y	J	T	N	J	M	C	D	L	E	V	B
S	A	T	H	U	M	I	D	I	T	Y	Y	V	G	C	V	E	O	T	Z	M	U	L
A	B	S	O	L	U	T	E	Z	E	R	O	T	E	M	P	E	R	A	T	U	R	E

1. The difference between the Dew Point and the Bubble Point.
2. Reducing contaminants in the used refrigerant
3. A passive throttling device, comprised of a small opening, located upstream of the evaporator.
4. The heart or "pump" within an air conditioning or heat pump system.
5. States that the volume occupied by a gas at a constant Pressure is directly proportional to the absolute temperature.
6. Unit used for measuring relative loudness of sounds.
7. Unit of measure referring to the flow of electrons within a circuit.
8. Either a sling type, or electronic. Instrument used to determine wet bulb temperatures and relative humidity.
9. The moving of heat from an undesirable location, to that of a location where its presence is less undesirable.
10. The process of extracting any air, non-condensable gases, or water from the system.
11. Tubing used in refrigeration which has ends to keep tubing clean and dry.
12. The total amount of moisture in air.
13. Side by side and having the same distance continuously between them.
14. Low pressure
15. A tool that measures pressure readings at different points in the refrigeration system.
16. Temperature at which molecular motion ceases.
17. The Gaseous state of any kind of matter that normally exists as a liquid or solid.
18. Forming a homogeneous mixture of liquids when added together.

A. Gauge manifold
D. Charles Law
G. Parallel
J. Refrigeration
M. Blue
P. Recycle

B. Absolute Zero Temperature
E. Decibel
H. Compressor
K. Psychrometer
N. Vapor
Q. ACR Tubing

C. Orifice Plate
F. Ampere
I. Miscible
L. Humidity
O. Temperature Glide
R. Evacuation

133

J. Find the hidden words. The words have been placed horizontally, vertically, or diagonally. When you locate a word, draw an ellipse around it.

```
D  I  S  T  I  L  L  A  T  I  O  N  P  E  P  R  V  Y  X  D  V  M  I
X  S  N  X  G  J  L  A  T  E  N  T  H  E  A  T  E  S  I  Z  B  A  N
P  Q  R  G  A  S  Z  U  P  T  E  S  A  U  T  A  L  P  Y  X  Y  N  S
I  F  X  E  W  L  P  A  S  S  I  V  E  R  E  C  O  V  E  R  Y  O  U
N  L  E  O  S  G  X  D  B  K  X  A  T  C  W  O  C  S  I  U  U  M  L
C  A  U  P  W  A  N  F  X  J  B  X  C  P  A  H  I  L  O  M  O  E  A
H  M  W  C  Z  S  R  E  F  R  I  G  E  R  A  N  T  C  R  N  I  T  T
O  E  H  S  G  A  C  C  U  M  U  L  A  T  O  R  Y  R  X  L  W  E  I
F  T  P  C  S  A  F  E  T  Y  P  L  U  G  D  D  H  O  Z  Y  Y  R  O
F  E  Q  I  V  G  Y  V  W  T  B  A  C  K  P  R  E  S  S  U  R  E  N
T  S  H  O  J  Z  V  F  V  S  D  B  O  F  N  Q  A  R  D  L  G  Z  T
O  T  S  E  R  V  I  C  E  M  A  N  I  F  O  L  D  Y  D  I  Z  M  H
O  H  E  A  D  P  R  E  S  S  U  R  E  C  O  N  T  R  O  L  Q  Y  E
U  M  Q  G  L  P  M  K  Y  Y  D  N  M  B  K  H  L  Z  N  K  S  L  R
S  A  T  U  R  A  T  I  O  N  T  E  M  P  E  R  A  T  U  R  E  Z  M
R  S  U  S  W  Y  P  Z  P  X  J  X  T  E  M  S  M  B  U  O  R  N  P
```

1. Heat energy absorbed in process of changing form of substance without change in temperature or pressure.
2. In flowing fluid, height of fluid equivalent to its velocity pressure.
3. Quantity of heat equivalent to 100,000 Btu.
4. Tool which is principally a torch and when an air refrigerant mixture is fed to flame, this flame will change color in presence of heated copper.
5. The form of matter that is an easily compressible fluid
6. Requires the assistance of components such as the appliance or unit's compressor to remove the refrigerant from the appliance.
7. Pressure operated control which opens electrical circuit if high side pressure becomes excessive.
8. Pressure in low side of refrigerating system; also called suction pressure or low side pressure.
9. The action of purifying a liquid by a process of heating and cooling.
10. The temperature where a refrigerant exists in both liquid and vapor form relative to its measured pressure.
11. Vapor phase or state of a substance.
12. Device used to press walls of a tubing together until fluid flow ceases.
13. A device equipped with gauges and manual valves, used by serviceman to service refrigerating systems.
14. Instrument to measuring pressure of gases and vapors.
15. The fluid used for heat transfer in a refrigeration system, which absorbs heat during evaporation at low temperature and pressure, and releases heat during condensation.
16. Any material or substance which has the ability to retard the flow or transfer of heat.
17. Device which releases the contents of a container above normal pressures, and before rupture pressures are reached.
18. Accumulates any low pressure liquid from the evaporator so it can vaporize before entering the compressor

A. Refrigerant	B. Therm	C. Back Pressure
D. Gas	E. Pinch off Tool	F. Flame Test
G. Distillation	H. Insulation	I. Safety Plug
J. Manometer	K. Accumulator	L. Service Manifold
M. Saturation Temperature	N. Latent Heat	O. Head Pressure Control
P. Gas	Q. Velocity Head	R. Passive recovery

K. Find the hidden words. The words have been placed horizontally, vertically, or diagonally. When you locate a word, draw an ellipse around it.

Z	E	A	D	I	A	B	A	T	I	C	C	O	M	P	R	E	S	S	I	O	N	O
Q	H	A	L	I	D	E	R	E	F	R	I	G	E	R	A	N	T	S	S	I	M	C
X	N	N	Y	O	Q	M	E	T	E	R	I	N	G	D	E	V	I	C	E	W	Q	M
J	A	C	C	U	M	U	L	A	T	O	R	Z	O	Q	C	E	R	C	Y	G	B	I
A	B	S	O	L	U	T	E	P	R	E	S	S	U	R	E	X	W	H	D	E	C	V
A	A	V	E	L	O	C	I	T	Y	H	E	A	D	V	N	H	H	X	I	R	D	U
B	C	L	H	S	K	F	F	Y	C	P	L	I	F	A	S	Z	Z	W	F	A	X	N
S	C	T	U	T	B	K	T	A	Q	F	U	L	U	P	I	J	F	M	F	H	L	V
O	E	R	M	A	U	L	X	A	E	L	X	P	Q	O	O	E	D	Z	U	N	J	T
R	L	D	I	T	P	S	B	L	T	A	L	M	H	R	G	B	C	T	S	L	O	D
B	E	F	D	I	F	M	E	X	P	A	N	S	I	O	N	D	E	V	I	C	E	Q
E	R	S	I	C	X	Z	V	C	H	A	R	L	E	S	L	A	W	K	O	Z	Q	P
N	A	I	T	H	V	V	Z	M	N	I	T	R	O	G	E	N	I	S	N	S	T	F
T	T	A	Y	E	L	M	O	W	F	R	E	F	R	I	G	E	R	A	N	T	V	N
X	E	D	Q	A	Z	T	H	X	A	C	I	D	C	O	N	D	I	T	I	O	N	C
K	R	T	G	D	A	S	M	A	L	L	A	P	P	L	I	A	N	C	E	T	J	V

1. In flowing fluid, height of fluid equivalent to its velocity pressure.
2. Creates pressure drop to allow liquid refrigerant to boil and absorb latent heat.
3. Pressure of fluid expressed in terms of height of column of the fluid, such as water or mercury.
4. The total amount of moisture in air.
5. The process whereby a gas spreads out through another gas to occupy the space with uniform partial Pressure.
6. Condition in which refrigerant and
7. Gas used for leak detection.
8. The Gaseous state of any kind of matter that normally exists as a liquid or solid.
9. Storage tank which receives liquid refrigerant from evaporator and prevents it from flowing into suction line.
10. States that the volume occupied by a gas at a constant Pressure is directly proportional to the absolute temperature.
11. A substance produces a refrigerating or cooling effect while expanding or vaporizing.
12. Family of refrigerants containing halogen chemicals.
13. Substance with ability to take up, or absorb another substance.
14. Gauge pressure plus atmospheric pressure (14.7 lbs. per sq. in.).
15. Converts high pressure liquid to low pressure vapor
16. Any products that are fully manufactured, charged, and hermetically sealed in a factory with five pounds or less of refrigerant
17. Compressing refrigerant gas without removing or adding heat.
18. To add to speed; hasten progress of development.

A. Accelerate
E. Diffusion
I. Adiabatic Compression
M. Accumulator
Q. Expansion device

B. Absorbent
F. Metering Device
J. Acid Condition
N. Halide Refrigerants
R. Small appliance

C. Humidity
G. Nitrogen
K. Velocity Head
O. Refrigerant

D. Absolute Pressure
H. Vapor
L. Static Head
P. Charles Law

135

L. Find the hidden words. The words have been placed horizontally, vertically, or diagonally. When you locate a word, draw an ellipse around it.

```
D  M  L  C  P  K  S  V  S  M  A  L  L  A  P  P  L  I  A  N  C  E  J
Z  P  E  B  E  E  B  T  Z  X  C  N  Z  I  B  N  C  K  Y  A  Z  N  F
H  A  B  Q  K  J  U  T  X  R  E  F  R  I  G  E  R  A  T  I  O  N  N
L  S  V  A  D  I  A  B  A  T  I  C  C  O  M  P  R  E  S  S  I  O  N
Q  S  U  C  V  X  G  Q  Z  G  D  Q  V  V  U  K  X  Z  F  M  R  V  W
T  I  U  R  E  C  O  V  E  R  Y  E  C  O  N  I  M  I  Z  E  R  X  Z
E  V  T  E  M  P  E  R  A  T  U  R  E  G  L  I  D  E  N  T  R  Y  G
S  E  D  Z  P  O  H  M  M  E  T  E  R  C  E  O  F  F  C  Y  C  L  E
T  R  I  S  H  K  T  H  E  R  M  O  S  T  A  T  G  M  R  K  A  G  O
L  E  F  C  Q  S  T  O  R  A  G  E  C  Y  L  I  N  D  E  R  S  F  P
I  C  F  U  Q  Z  W  T  S  B  T  H  E  A  D  P  R  E  S  S  U  R  E
G  O  U  Z  U  Z  F  I  N  D  U  C  T  I  O  N  M  O  T  O  R  W  N
H  V  S  J  N  Y  B  A  D  B  T  R  C  D  N  S  T  U  G  V  P  S  I
T  E  I  G  T  M  O  N  T  R  E  A  L  P  R  O  T  O  C  O  L  T  N
D  R  O  S  C  M  H  N  I  E  Y  H  E  K  C  E  L  Z  F  Y  O  M  G
C  Y  N  N  W  A  T  M  O  S  P  H  E  R  E  J  B  Z  G  M  E  E  H
```

1. An instrument for measuring resistance in ohms.
2. Compressing refrigerant gas without removing or adding heat.
3. A temperature control device. Typically mounted in conditioned space.
4. Pressure which exists in condensing side of refrigerating system.
5. The difference between the Dew Point and the Bubble Point.
6. Larger cylinders used for storing refrigerant to be transferred to smaller refillable cylinders.
7. An AC motor which operates on principle of rotating magnetic field. Rotor has no electrical connection, but receives electrical energy by transformer action from field windings.
8. The process whereby a gas spreads out through another gas to occupy the space with uniform partial Pressure.
9. Light provided with test leads, used to test or probe electrical circuits to determine if they are alive.
10. Treaty among nations designed to protect the stratospheric ozone layer.
11. Any products that are fully manufactured, charged, and hermetically sealed in a factory with five pounds or less of refrigerant
12. A mechanism that removes flash gas from the evaporator.
13. Requires the assistance of components such as the appliance or unit's compressor to remove the refrigerant from the appliance.
14. The process of collecting used refrigerant.
15. A unit of Pressure equal to exactly 760 mmHg
16. That time period of a refrigeration cycle when the system is not operating.
17. Any maintenance or repair on an appliance that would release refrigerant from the appliance to the atmosphere.
18. The process of cooling or chilling.

A. Passive recovery
B. Head Pressure
C. Test Light
D. Thermostat
E. Econimizer
F. Induction Motor
G. Storage cylinders
H. Small appliance
I. Ohmmeter
J. Refrigeration
K. Opening
L. Temperature Glide
M. Atmosphere
N. Recovery
O. Off Cycle
P. Montreal Protocol
Q. Adiabatic Compression
R. Diffusion

M. Find the hidden words. The words have been placed horizontally, vertically, or diagonally. When you locate a word, draw an ellipse around it.

Y	C	Q	D	I	S	P	O	S	A	B	L	E	C	Y	L	I	N	D	E	R	S	O
K	G	H	Y	D	R	O	S	T	A	T	I	C	Z	O	V	O	K	N	E	V	I	F
A	H	Q	C	H	L	O	R	I	N	E	Q	V	W	J	T	S	H	Q	P	W	S	F
Z	K	I	T	E	M	P	E	R	A	T	U	R	E	G	L	I	D	E	H	W	Z	C
E	T	A	F	I	F	R	A	C	T	I	O	N	A	T	I	O	N	L	U	F	A	Y
O	R	C	A	B	P	J	A	A	T	I	Q	R	I	V	N	G	V	A	U	K	G	C
T	D	N	G	O	N	K	U	C	Z	F	V	Q	W	S	R	R	F	A	G	V	S	L
R	T	E	S	T	L	I	G	H	T	Q	Z	Q	F	E	F	F	U	S	I	O	N	E
O	S	M	A	L	L	A	P	P	L	I	A	N	C	E	R	Y	N	Z	M	K	Z	U
P	T	N	P	V	A	C	U	U	M	C	O	N	T	R	O	L	S	Y	S	T	E	M
H	S	A	T	U	R	A	T	I	O	N	T	E	M	P	E	R	A	T	U	R	E	T
R	E	F	R	I	G	E	R	A	T	I	O	N	N	C	O	H	M	M	E	T	E	R
A	B	S	O	L	U	T	E	Z	E	R	O	T	E	M	P	E	R	A	T	U	R	E
Y	G	X	V	A	C	U	U	M	P	U	M	P	U	D	U	B	L	C	W	P	Q	A
R	E	C	E	I	V	E	R	H	E	A	T	I	N	G	E	L	E	M	E	N	T	O
G	A	S	P	N	M	N	Q	J	V	M	H	D	N	U	W	V	C	E	C	X	R	Y

1. The difference between the Dew Point and the Bubble Point.
2. The form of matter that is an easily compressible fluid
3. A mixture of at least two different liquids.
4. That time period of a refrigeration cycle when the system is not operating.
5. In some air conditioning systems, vacuum is used to operate dampers and controls in system.
6. Special high efficiency device (pump) used create deep vacuum within an AC
7. Any products that are fully manufactured, charged, and hermetically sealed in a factory with five pounds or less of refrigerant
8. A separation process in which a certain quantity of a mixture is divided during a phase transition
9. Single use cylinders. Empty cylinders should have the pressure reduced to zero and the cylinder rendered unusable.
10. Light provided with test leads, used to test or probe electrical circuits to determine if they are alive.
11. The temperature where a refrigerant exists in both liquid and vapor form relative to its measured pressure.
12. The atom found in CFC and HCFC refrigerants that destroys ozone in the stratosphere.
13. The process of cooling or chilling.
14. Temperature at which molecular motion ceases.
15. The process in which a gas flows through a small hole in a container.
16. Electrical resistance mounted in or around liquid receiver, used to maintain head pressures when ambient temperature is at freezing or below freezing.
17. An instrument for measuring resistance in ohms.
18. A form of testing for high pressure cylinders.

A. Temperature Glide
D. Refrigeration
G. Effusion
J. Absolute Zero Temperature
M. Hydrostatic
P. Small appliance

B. Ohmmeter
E. Vacuum Control System
H. Disposable cylinders
K. Chlorine
N. Off Cycle
Q. Saturation Temperature

C. Gas
F. Fractionation
I. Test Light
L. Azeotroph
O. Vacuum Pump
R. Receiver Heating Element

N. Find the hidden words. The words have been placed horizontally, vertically, or diagonally. When you locate a word, draw an ellipse around it.

E	V	A	P	O	R	A	T	O	R	C	O	I	L	P	I	S	T	O	N	H	P	V
W	W	V	D	G	V	Q	J	V	K	L	F	I	G	H	A	B	D	J	E	G	M	Y
T	G	I	Y	F	J	Y	T	R	Y	B	G	S	A	A	S	P	Q	U	H	V	F	P
C	Q	Q	T	R	K	K	Q	W	D	A	B	O	U	L	N	R	V	N	Y	Q	B	Q
O	O	W	Y	W	W	W	S	X	I	F	A	L	E	O	L	O	L	C	D	K	I	Y
N	R	V	A	P	O	R	V	H	Z	P	C	A	Y	N	E	O	O	T	R	N	V	B
D	A	D	S	O	R	P	T	I	O	N	K	T	T	X	A	L	J	I	O	L	J	A
E	Q	Z	C	Y	H	S	T	T	B	U	P	E	B	F	K	L	H	O	C	S	Q	C
N	M	O	A	Z	I	C	B	Q	I	J	R	J	B	D	R	U	L	N	A	Y	T	K
S	L	A	T	E	N	T	H	E	A	T	E	V	Y	L	A	I	J	B	R	R	Y	S
E	C	O	X	U	W	I	D	F	D	D	S	K	X	J	T	M	B	O	B	N	Y	E
R	T	H	E	R	M	O	S	T	A	T	S	M	P	X	E	I	S	X	O	Q	G	A
C	I	H	E	A	D	P	R	E	S	S	U	R	E	C	L	Q	J	G	N	H	C	T
O	W	B	W	U	E	G	T	Z	G	E	R	S	U	P	E	R	H	E	A	T	Y	I
I	A	K	O	P	R	E	F	R	I	G	E	R	A	T	I	O	N	H	T	K	N	N
U	V	U	U	Q	K	Y	Q	M	T	W	V	A	C	U	U	M	G	A	U	G	E	G

1. cause to be or remain alone or apart from others.
2. A chemical used in fire extinguishing.
3. Close fitting part which moves up and down in a cylinder.
4. The adhesion of a thin layer of molecules of a gas or liquid to a solid object.
5. Dissipates heat from the refrigerant.
6. Pressure in low side of refrigerating system; also called suction pressure or low side pressure.
7. Heat energy absorbed in process of changing form of substance without change in temperature or pressure.
8. A temperature control device. Typically mounted in conditioned space.
9. The temperature rise within an evaporator or suction line assembly from the evaporator's saturation temperature.
10. The process of cooling or chilling.
11. Group of electrical terminals housed in protective box or container.
12. Pressure which exists in condensing side of refrigerating system.
13. The Gaseous state of any kind of matter that normally exists as a liquid or solid.
14. The rate at which an appliance is losing refrigerant.
15. Where heat is absorbed by warm air passing across. Liquid refrigerant boils as it is metered into coil, and changes from liquid to vapor.
16. A compound containing only the elements hydrogen and carbon.
17. Instrument used to measure pressures below atmospheric pressure.
18. Fluid opening

A. Head Pressure	B. Super Heat	C. Vacuum Gauge	D. Evaporator Coil	E. Piston
F. Back Seating	G. Adsorption	H. Thermostat	I. Condenser Coil	J. Vapor
K. Leak Rate	L. Refrigeration	M. Junction Box	N. Hydrocarbon	O. Latent Heat
P. Back Pressure	Q. Isolate	R. Halon		

O. Find the hidden words. The words have been placed horizontally, vertically, or diagonally. When you locate a word, draw an ellipse around it.

M	V	W	V	I	A	H	P	F	R	A	C	T	I	O	N	A	T	I	O	N	H	M
A	B	S	O	L	U	T	E	Z	E	R	O	T	E	M	P	E	R	A	T	U	R	E
J	S	S	P	F	I	E	L	D	P	O	L	E	R	E	T	P	W	U	N	E	W	T
Z	T	M	I	C	L	M	W	E	V	A	P	O	R	A	T	O	R	C	O	I	L	E
N	T	Z	D	T	I	B	F	B	N	I	R	M	B	U	C	E	C	M	Q	I	T	R
R	A	C	T	I	V	E	R	E	C	O	V	E	R	Y	G	S	Q	W	D	I	Z	I
Y	V	C	K	V	Y	V	E	L	O	C	I	T	Y	H	E	A	D	S	M	X	V	N
R	K	U	R	E	F	R	I	G	E	R	A	N	T	C	I	R	C	U	I	T	G	G
E	M	J	Y	D	A	M	P	E	R	Y	J	D	D	Z	Z	W	N	T	C	T	L	D
I	N	S	U	L	A	T	I	O	N	D	M	U	Y	W	C	P	M	P	C	F	W	E
J	S	C	O	M	P	R	E	S	S	O	R	C	F	Q	Y	Y	Z	L	C	F	G	V
X	F	Z	V	Y	W	G	W	B	W	Z	B	T	K	I	N	G	V	A	L	V	E	I
P	I	N	C	H	O	F	F	T	O	O	L	W	U	J	T	N	S	Q	R	X	H	C
S	B	Z	A	C	C	U	M	U	L	A	T	O	R	L	U	I	X	P	U	Q	R	E
F	W	O	T	X	G	Q	Q	J	R	E	F	R	I	G	E	R	A	N	T	F	E	A
K	Q	T	E	C	H	N	I	C	I	A	N	K	M	A	N	O	M	E	T	E	R	K

1. The parts of an appliance that are normally connected to each other and are designed to contain refrigerant.
2. The fluid used for heat transfer in a refrigeration system, which absorbs heat during evaporation at low temperature and pressure, and releases heat during condensation.
3. In flowing fluid, height of fluid equivalent to its velocity pressure.
4. Round or rectangular pipes or controlled paths acting as conduit for return, mixed, makeup, supply or exhaust air.
5. Temperature at which molecular motion ceases.
6. Where heat is absorbed by warm air passing across. Liquid refrigerant boils as it is metered into coil, and changes from liquid to vapor.
7. A combination shut-off and service value typically used on the inlet and outlet of a compressor.
8. Any material or substance which has the ability to retard the flow or transfer of heat.
9. Part of stator of motor which concentrates magnetic field of field winding.
10. Any person who performs maintenance, service, or repair that could reasonably be expected to release class I or class II substances into the atmosphere.
11. Valve for controlling airflow. Found in duct work, movable plate opens and closes to control airflow.
12. Storage tank which receives liquid refrigerant from evaporator and prevents it from flowing into suction line.
13. Instrument to measuring pressure of gases and vapors.
14. Equipment that has its own compressor or pump.
15. Creates pressure drop to allow liquid refrigerant to boil and absorb latent heat.
16. Device used to press walls of a tubing together until fluid flow ceases.
17. The heart or "pump" within an air conditioning or heat pump system.
18. A separation process in which a certain quantity of a mixture is divided during a phase transition

A. Pinch off Tool
D. Absolute Zero Temperature
G. Field Pole
J. Metering Device
M. Evaporator Coil
P. Refrigerant circuit

B. Velocity Head
E. Compressor
H. Ductwork
K. Technician
N. Refrigerant
Q. King Valve

C. Accumulator
F. Fractionation
I. Damper
L. Manometer
O. Insulation
R. Active recovery

139

Made in the USA
Monee, IL
24 September 2019